Unlock

Your Hidden

Powers

Michael U. Mbuko

Unlock Your Hidden Powers

Copyright © 2015 Michael U. Mbuko

Tel: +234-8091653017, +234-8064308507

Email: michaelmbuko@gmail.com

First Published by Chiysonovelty International 2015

ISBN: 9785033767
ISBN-13: 978-9785033762

Chiysonovelty International

Plot 8 Evule Avenue

Aba,

Nigeria

Email: chiyson@minister.com

Phone: 234-818-118-3131

Printed in the United States of America

To God Be the Glory, Great Things He has done.

DEDICATION

This book is dedicated to my Mom and Dad who had patience on me when I was a little boy desperately cutting my school books to write stories and bind them together with needle and thread trying to create a book I can call my own.

"Try to create a space in your mind for thoughts majorly on the "big you" from there will you draw energy to help you on the "now" moment to reflect your action."

- Michael U. Mbuko

CONTENTS

Dedication IV

Acknowledgments VII

Preface 1

1 Who are You? Pg #3

2 The Powerhouse Pg #24

3 Upgrade Your Mind Pg #39

4 The Powerhouse Virus Pg #47

5 Will Power Pg #59

6 Emotional Intelligence Pg #69

7 Favour Factor Pg #90

8 Take the Lead Pg #116

9 Behavioral Power Pg #139

10 Power of love Pg #156

About the Book Pg #176

About the Author Pg #178

ACKNOWLEDGMENTS

Firstly, I have to appreciate God for the gift of writing; I also appreciate James Cerulean Adelaja for helping me see how precious this gift is; I have come to acknowledge my parents who provided a conducive environment for me to learn, unlearn and to re-learn.

I say a big thank you to Emenike Odinaka a Co-founder of CYLPI, I appreciate Mirable Chynwa, Mercy Uchendu, Deborah Edom, Chiemela, Alice Tonia, Oge Boniface, Chukwuemeka Okafor, Peace, Janeth, Blessing Nnaji, Dike and many other CYLPI members: who dedicated their time and money to make the Less-privileged better.

I also acknowledge my room mates who made my final year at the University an interesting one and also contributed to the success of this book, in the person of Michael Ovie, Tope, Tony, Rotimi, Sheyi Adejumo and my lovely brother and friend Adekunle Adewumi, I also want to acknowledge Fabian Jachinma, Joyce Mbuko, Stella Lekwauwa and Gabriel who was awesome.

I wouldn't want to forget Kenny for his care. Let me seize this opportunity to thank Tony Joy the National Co-ordinator of "*We Are Mad*" Initiative for editing this piece. Let me also acknowledge Chiyson Sam Anyaele who gave me an opportunity to write my name in the list of authors.

I won't fail to acknowledge my sister: Gift Mbuko, my brothers: Roland, Samuel, Lawrence, Chukwuemeka and Rich Mbuko for their Kind gestures and also Trisha, Blessing Ikpeama; Joy and Blessing Mbuko for their undying love for me. Let me thank my ultimate mentor: Happy James, and Mr Edwin Amadi for sticking around to motivate us all, I can't forget Mr Edwin usually tells me that *"Roman wasn't build in a day."*

I won't forget to remember Prince Ice, Godwin, Peter, Unique and James who allowed me to learn from them and also Mr Awosonya and Mrs Linda Alade for their care. I'm grateful to my students: Sunday, Deborah, Kemi, Demilola; Victoria Olabisi and Sheyi Oluwole my wonderful friends.

Let me appreciate my friends in the Philippines and Hongkong most especially Hazel and Victoria Adelantar. I also appreciate Faith Ndubisi my long term friend and also Lilian Anyanwu for her motivation, also Hollywood Photographs for a clean shot. If am to continue, I will write a book on acknowledgment; even those I didn't mention, I remembered you but had limited space. Bear with me!

PREFACE

World powers are aware that whoever controls technology controls the world, may be that is the reason they are concerned about any human innovations around the world. No wonder Roman Empire ruled the world because they built roads; the British Empire ruled the world because they built ships, the Americans the atomic bomb.

Personally, you can rule your own world if you control the technologies within you. If you realize who you are, that is, the complex technical wiring and wireless complex of the soul and the brain and the power in its possession then will you be able to use them to your advantage to control the outside world and become the best the world is waiting to manifest.

Draw out the best of yourself because inherent in you are abilities you ever imagine, it leverages you and makes you active and extra-ordinary. You might have unconsciously programmed yourself to function in a certain way since you were a kid to adulthood, but the truth is that you are much more than that if you can believe in something big and walk under the truth revealed in this book.

We have capacity to be what we want to be , but most times we lack the light to show the way. Reading this book with an open mind will guide you through the world so dark to that bright city of your destiny, it can become the golden cape that will aid you fly to endless possibilities.

This master piece guarantees you timeless strategies to a golden future. With THESE, if you can`t be the favorite then become the second favorite but celebrate the magical moments from now on, internalize the concepts and make things flow naturally, that's the reason you are natures Nano machine as this book will give you the ability to bounce back better and sound.

You are not far away FROM THE unlocking process. Just keep unlocking and own the ability to recreate the entire universe your own way. Accept the fact that you are remarkable; thrive on your remarkable human gifts.

They are there waiting to be discovered and to be used by no one but you and start changing anything you want to change, you have the power. Our examples are drawn from remarkable people who had stood out in there various societies. Each particular chapter is solving a problem and my philosophy is that any book that is not of impact is not worthy to be called a book.

CHAPTER ONE

WHO ARE YOU?
IDENTITY

It is almost certain that most of us don't know who we are, but it is true that it is only when you know who you are that you will be able to fathom your full potential.

For Munroe Myle, once said that the treasures of this world is heaped at the cemeteries all over the world, making it the world most wealthiest place. It will be saddening to know that most of us don't know who we are.

If you don't know who you are, it is like living with a clock with no battery, staying at a fixed POINT the rest of your life. If you don't know who you are, you can't know where you are going; you can't move forward rather you will be dwindling. It becomes glaring that you will live in fear, and fear will always be a poor chisel that do carve out the tomorrow of those who don't know who they are. The tragedy of life is not just losing the battle; it is not just failing in an activity. It is not just being sidelined in life; it is all about knowing who you are.

If you don't know who you are then you can't draw the unlimited wealth from the Universal mind. It is only when you know who you are will you have what to say about yourself even to your admirers.

DISCOVER YOURSELF

"Why sit down there and cry
Don't you know you represent a star in the sky?
It's high time you polish it
So get all your cleaning kit."

You cannot love and hold if you don't know who you are. You cannot blaze the trail; you cannot engrave your name in gold, if you don't know who you are.

How can you plant your footprint in the sands of time if you don't know who you are? You can't wait for the London bridge to close before you cross. *"the truth (about yourself) will make you free"* Jesus.

Russ Von observed in his book *"How to achieve total success"* that within the wonderful word *"aware"* there is the word *"ARE."* Anyone who wants to excel in all they do must firstly reach the realization of who they are.

It is only on knowing who you are, will you open up the mind that can do all things and also open up to new perspective and become the best you truly are, then start on the *"now"* moment, bear in mind that everything you are is just the state of your mind.

Without the mind you are just without ideas, no past, no future--- this is the secret of the ages, the secret which made William Shakespeare write masterpieces, the secret behind Michael Angelo's Mona Lisa (*painting*), the idea behind Karl Marx's communism and the brain behind Napoleon's success across the sea.

YOU CAN SEE THAT IT BOILS DOWN TO THE THOUGHTS WHICH ENTERS THE MIND THEN COMES OUT OF THE MOUTH AND THEN FINALLY SHAPES THE CHARACTER. Many like me will agree with Rene Descartes that *"what you think-you are"*

IDENTIFY YOUR IDENTITY

THINK

"To learn how to think is to learn how to know" What you think is who you are, it all begins with thought, it would be agreed that a mind that cannot think is a dead mind and is not worthy of existences I was able to identify *two* types of thinking, which are: *Shallow thinking* and *Deep thinking*.

Shallow thinking: Shallow thinking is actually the minor thoughts that don't add to you but are to some extent important most especially in decision making. They are the thoughts for quick decision making like wanting to know whether it is necessary to call your mum today while you called her yesterday. Those thoughts when you think whether it's right to drink water or not, like thoughts of going to give Junior a peck or not. These are shallow thoughts.

Deep Thoughts: These are those thoughts that you think deeply and are also referred to as meditation. It plays the role of deep thinking and are focus on the *"now"* moment. It involves concentration and attention, you start by taking a deep breath and realizing it to clear the mind, then think about the plans, project or package but don't allow unproductive thoughts to drift in, maintain your concentration in all distraction.

Deep thoughts open you up to new ideas, broadens and awaken your consciousness about who you truly are. Though deep thinking can further be classified into productive and unproductive thinking. Productive thinking help you in taking drastic STEP to bring to reality today's real you.

Try to create a space in your mind for thoughts majorly on the "*big you*" from there will you draw energy to help you on the "*now*" moment to reflect your action. Never forget that what you think is who you are, so think big about yourself and no one can make you feel inferior.

What you think represents who you are, it reflects in your appearance, speech and reasoning. Create a big mental image about yourself and its picture in reality will baffle even you and people around you will be amazed to the wonderful you that they see.

LEARNING

Learning is part of human existence. To really identify who you are you have to take studying serious. Intensify your desire to study and allow the steamed fire from your eyes to burn the words into ashes, and then let the wind of awareness blow it to your already opened mind and you will develop a new level of consciousness.

To know who you are you need to study because you need to develop your mind which is significant to who you are because without the human mind the human is nothing, then that real you needs to gain new consciousness, it needs to be elevated because without the mind which control the body then such individual have no past, ideas, no future, no experience, no life.

Then that real you which is your intelligence needs to be developed and in so doing gain a new consciousness which translates to who you are. There are times we feed the body and leave nothing for the mind, feed the mind by learning something today and be amazed by the superior being you will become.

For starters these might not be easy but practice is the process and diligently practicing to learn will need some quantum of discipline; you will have to decide on the number of page you must read per day and stick to it or you will have to decide the minute or hour you will carve out of your 24hours to read. It won't be easy because its a new hobby then develop gradually as time goes.

SERVICE

"Service is the path way to greatness."

Lose yourself into service of others; it makes your potential come alive just like a renewed body on a dead bone and also breathe life into them. Service to humanity brings you out for people to see.

When you render your service to humanity there and then will you notice the activity that well defines you, and also will you get to find out the activity that you're best in and engage into stress free and also will you point out the one you derive joy in and have the comparative advantage in.

While into service you'll make mistakes, correct them and get better because mistakes are second chance to get better but don't forget that what defines you is your patience when you have nothing and your attitude when you have it all then discover yourself by discipline, in service to humanity. Take up positions in church, school and your work place, aim towards influencing decisions{*POSITIVELY*}and you will discover yourself in the process.

THEN WHO ARE YOU?

Look at how precious you are that the earth delight to feel your bare feet, the winds long to play with your hair, the birds are glad to sing for you Russ Von.

The Master Craft created us all a little different, but that difference makes a whole lot of difference, He loves variety. He is not weird neither did he create you by mistake; you are a unique being and you are the only original with the greatest value. You are more than mere copies of something else.

Don't compare yourself with others and spend your life competing with people while you can stand out. For we dare not class ourselves or compare ourselves with those who commend themselves, you are the spice that sweeten this world, you're an artist, anchor and treasure that activates the world, you are the corner stone, one out of the seven billion human heads in the world.

The world is not well spelt without you. Its only you that can say and shape who you are so don't go home asking for who you are because home is not only where you live rather it is where the people there understands who you are because your personality supersedes the color of your skin, but beneath your skin, Underneath those skins lies something so glaring and bright.

The reason you've not seen it all this while might be because you haven't taken your ample time to rigorously look within, you've always been conscious with the happenings on the outside.

The reason you brood over your past years is just because you have not taken your time to define who you are, the true you is not the outside, it is the inside, it does so many things for you and it is the mind, it takes care of the subconscious and the conscious, the subconscious consist 90% of who you are while the outside which is the conscious completes the remaining 100%.

It is the only sense that exists even if the rest is not functional but some of us neglect this great biological factory which constitute who we are, the powerhouse that attracts great things to you.

Mind connects and that's the reason you ARE ABLE TO IDENTIFY with like minds. Your mind takes care of your breathe even while you are asleep, it works wonders you don't even know, it takes care of you overtime even when you're injured because it stimulates the nerves and vein in charge of replacing a worn out tissue.

It takes care of the pumping heart, it directs the blood and water that flows through your nerves, veins and ligaments. It feeds on the intake of the five senses. Imagine the valuable thing you've got then look carefully, think straight and you will realize that within you is a king, the world ruler.

The President within you awaits discovery, you possess a kingly nature and personality remember it takes you to think like one then a signal will be sent to your subconscious mind which help you bring it into reality.

First black President of America became the world President when he made up his mind to become one. What you are and what you desire is within you, you don't need to go to Saudi Arabia, Canada, United Arab Emirate, Japan or even United States to get it; you can only make a choice to go just to get yourself sharpened.

Deposit within you is an acre of diamond lying crude untapped surprisingly it is the world richest site all you have to do is to discover it, explore and prosper.

You are one of the lords on earth, the priestly anointing, the sonship carriage, a *bonafide* owner of the whole universe. Just take your time to reason out how reflex action takes place, or even imagine the intricate complexities in human brain then will you realize that you are a miracle to the world.

Take another moment to look beyond your skin color, race, family background, financial status, religious discrepancies, what people call you and where you reside.

It is about the Universal Mind who has given you unlimited wealth, unconditional love. He had done great work in you and expects even greater creativity from you. You don't believe all these because i wrote so but because your manufacturer said you are so.

It doesn't matter how shattered you think your past might have been, look up to the real you because you are a reflection of what you see in your mind's eye.

Firstly renew your mind with great thoughts that will shape your character and build greatly on your future then learn to believe on the new you though it will take some time before people gets convince about the most capable you but always remember not to give up and don't forget that you believe in yourself before people gets to believe in you, the world wants to be convicted about you before believing in you.

The only way to convince the world is to keep being who you are and not impatiently giving up on yourself suddenly because of probably circumstances that surround you.

Value yourself: In our present world present yourself like a product no matter how much you know your packaging speaks volume.

Am not advising you spend your money on clothes but you've got to dress well because you're addressed by the way you dress. Then your carriage also speaks for you. The other thing that adds to your value is self-respect.

When you respect yourself then will people respect you and value you. If you can see yourself as a king, superstar, the best among all then go ahead to become it. Knowing it is the first step of becoming it.

It doesn't matter if you are the only one that knows yourself with time other people will know. Never forget that the time is now. You no longer have to keep the whole world waiting, human race awaits your manifestation so don't see yourself merely how you appear now, you may have an old laptop, live in an old apartment or may not even have any job, you may even have a health problem but they are not a true reflection of who you are as long as you are working on a vision that has a target.

Good, bad, terrific, worse or even tough are all a state of mind, these are what enters your heart and you think about them constantly in your subconscious and they reflects in your emotions in so doing shape what is now you and shape your actions and what you say in a given time.

For example during time of war we sense threat by the knowledge of what bullets, grenades and nuclear weapon can do then we begin to think about its effect on the economy which determines our next action.

But when you convince yourself that in spite all these threats that your existence is not dependent on the society or even the environment you see yourself makes you a better person no wonder some people avoid the newspapers because you scarcely see mind boggling achievement or outstanding arts, science and technology.

We only see election fraud, chaos and crisis in our society which limit the level in which we go to open new doors for human spirits and new knowledge being unveiled.

It also limit the inspiration of new motivational stories about love, human kindness because what you read reflects who you are. Read books to inspire yourself to greatness because new leaders must rise and the whole world can't wait for too long so get started now.

You are created in God's image and likeness, God created the world, you too can create one too because you possess the image of the Universal Intelligent to create a new you.

No one can be found who has the same handwriting as you, no one has the same taste of food, music or art as you, no one laugh or cry like you, no one react to situations as you. You are not special by accident but the Infinite Intelligence deliberately made you to be like that. No wonder you are so priceless no matter how low, old or disgusting you feel.

You are wonderful that no amount can buy a piece of you then imagine how rich you're to own the whole you that is your entirely self. You are unique and it is that uniqueness that makes you special.

Remember the reason you are special is just because you are different not because you are like everybody. Now you have little or no point telling me how many ghosts that have risen in your ugly scenarios of the past and how they're haunting your present.

There is also no point folding your hands and blaming your parents for leaving no wealth behind when you possess what can attract wealth to you.

Why not step up your shine and take the lead by becoming master of your fate, the time is now. Find out the truth why it didn't WORK out the previous time then build on that fact and get better.

WHAT DO YOU WANT OUT OF LIFE?

Ifeoma Okoye, the President at Breast Without Spot (*BWS*) in Nigeria and UK and a consultant Radiologist at the University of Nigeria Teaching Hospital, Enugu, (*UNTH*) said *"My philosophy is that our purpose in life supersedes just getting married, having children, celebrating births and mourning deaths, we were all created with a true purpose and the onus is on each of us to find it and fulfill it."*

What are you saying, what do you want out of life? In order to thrive and encounter an unimaginable ends, you need to know what you want out of life.

In life needs and wants can be likely but aren't the same thing. Needs are your necessities but wants are your desires. You use your needs to get what you want and you can't desire except you know what you want then you have to know what you want in order to be desirable, valuable and creative, a sculptor can't cave out a wonderful figure without knowing what he want the wood for.

Jack wouldn't have meet Rose in the wonderful classic *"the titanic"* if he didn't know what he wanted. Not knowing what you wanted is the reason for life failures, failed marriages and broken relationship. This world is being propelled with the concept of want because it is only when you know what you want will you start making plans on how to get them, will you also have the propensity to think and to dream big.

Myles Munroe highlighted the third world as a category of people who for whatever reason have been robbed off the opportunity to discover, develop, define, release and maximize their God's given potentials.

The way out of this is to indulge into critical thinking on how to deal with the ugly monster that wants to devour everyone in the third world. When you know what you want, you aim for not only the stars but the entire universe, you just have to stamp your feet on the floor and blame no one for any misfortune that had stood on your way.

A man who doesn't know what he wants only remains in the mercy of luck, they are slaves to nature, slaves to hard work and slaves to humanity. Michael Faraday knew what he wanted which resulted to electricity.

Ts'aiLun knew what he wanted when he initiated a paper making process in about 105 C.E. It later lead to the mass production of paper. A man who doesn't know what he wants will be committed to working anywhere but knowing what you want is a precious thing for which independence is accompanied. It makes you creative, guides you to your plans and propels your hope for an unexpected end.

HOW TO FIGURE OUT WHAT YOU WANT

To figure out what you want takes you back to understudy who you are. Who you really are reveals what you would likely want and what you want propels your character. You are powerfully made by the creator and the Universal mind knows what you want. What you have to do is to meditate and pray to him because he can feed your mind with desires and the willpower to achieve them.

HOW TO GET WHAT YOU WANT

God gave us a world unfinished so we might share in the joy and satisfaction of creation

According to Wallace D. Wattles, *"To think health when surrounded by the appearances of disease or to think riches when in the midst of appearances of poverty, requires power, but he who acquires this power becomes a master mind. He can conquer fate; he can have what he wants."*

Deeply think on what you want, because in doing so will you attract what it takes to bring what you want to existence. Though you would have to spend some time collecting data, and Information that will be of help to you in order to bring your thoughts into reality.

This is the process of creation and in so doing you are creating yourself and shaping your character. Though conditions might not be favorable but what people want to hear is how we made it beyond all odds and I think that will make your story more readable.

YOUR PAST IS IN THE PAST

I want to encourage you to take quality time and study this quote, *"Your past is Your Experience, the present an experiment while your future is your expectation then use your experience in your experiments to get an expectation."* – Anonymous

You can only sail across the second ocean when you forget that you would've drowned in the first. Our past have a way of robbing us, they cloud our vision and make us dormant. It is now time to think about how to make yourself better by a collection of true facts from your past and amending your ways then avoid making similar mistake.

CHAPTER TWO
THE POWERHOUSE

YOU CANNOT BE HEALTHIER & WEALTHIER THAN YOUR MIND

Wouldn't you be the happiest man or woman in the world if i tell you how you have been unknowingly attracting those things that happened to you that you didn't like? I know you would be glad to know how to stop attracting those bad things if you are taught how to.

Nevertheless wouldn't you prefer to take the same process of attracting bad things to attract good things? You have a mind that serves as an agent to you, any thought you package in your heart is what reflects in your reality.

ALL THINGS BEGIN WITH A THOUGHT

To think is a letter short of thing simply explaining that what you think brings that thing in spite of what it is. Before you board that economic class you thought of so many things before being convicted to pay for the air ticket. That Disney Park came out of the thoughts of one man and not all men.

It took energy to creatively think those things out before it was actualized. Whatever that you can see came from the inside. Open your mind's eye with your thought and you can see that which no one has ever seen.

Though nothing is new on earth surface, but you can still UNRAVEL the mystery of the world with your mind's eye before the moves to bring them to reality. As you engage in creative thinking you can as well apply techniques required to bringing them all out.

Every society witness almost the same pattern of development which means that every society once used bow and arrow, even knives to fight before the age of atomic and chemical weapon, that doesn't mean that the people of that time have no potential to produce nuclear war head but it was to the extent their mental capacity can indulge in brought the weapon they used as of that time.

Now the required techniques which would be applied entails having a target, a definite goal, desire, belief and persistence in achieving your stated goal but you see, everything begins with your thoughts. Just as you create things with your thoughts, you can still create yourself be thinking.

Displaying a great thought about yourself help you create a great you. So if your thoughts can go 180 degrees, try making it 300 or above and you can write a masterpiece, invent an unknown machine or even advance a platform for GSM.

You can even design an appealing social media. It all begins in the thought. And there are forms of thinking which ARE worrying and meditation.

WORRY

Worrying is a form of thought but it is categorized as the negative THINKING. Worry is focusing your thoughts on your past failures, heartbreaks, sicknesses and disappointments etc. Worry makes your mind to dwell on the negatives just like planting weeds in the subconscious. Your subconscious will further attract that crisis that you dwell on.

I remember my friend bought a meal from the restaurant. (*HE HAD A NEGATIVE THOUGHT THAT*

THE FOOD COULD MAKE HIM PURGE) after eating the food HE had a running stomach. That's how powerful your thoughts are. But let's take in right things into the subconscious through meditation.

MEDITATION

Meditation is not difficult, its take the same form as *"worry."* In this context it entails dwelling on those positive thoughts. Meditation involves deep thinking of nice things that is or that is to come. Meditation is a known secret of success and happiness because it shapes your character, makes you better and sends positive SIGNALS to the subconscious to further attract.. {*IT IS INCREASINGLY APPRIASED AS IMPORTANT AS IT IS MADE RENOWNED IN COLLEGES AND UNIVERSITIES AS A PART OF THE SCHEME OF WORK*}

THE MIND

Student of mind science will agree with me that there is only one mind. We all are in possession of only one mind which performs dual functions. Each distinct characteristics is special to each other, they have separate attribute, function and powers.

These two functions of one mind are often referred to AS cause and effect. The effect which is the conscious and the other which is the cause is referred to as the subconscious.

THE CONSCIOUS MIND

The first mind function is the conscious mind. That's the state of which we operate WHICH we are aware of I.E OF WHAT WE ARE DOING. For instance you are aware that you are reading a book. The conscious mind responds to the senses, it is preoccupied with perceptions and feeling, pain and pleasure.

The conscious mind is an instrument of sensation; it relates to the world and responds to the world. Without self-direction your conscious mind can and does send all kinds of signals to your subconscious.

Some of these things can be positive while the other might be extremely negative. It's just like cropping a seed of corn and weed together in a land called subconscious. If you look constantly more into this principle, your new found law will positively shape your character that will transform your life to a new power, success and happiness.

Men who understand themselves act more cordial because they understand there conscious power, which enables them to be effective in lives battle.

They know when and when not to breath, and their smiles are coordinated, they use the mouth well and are affecting others positively but the causes begin in the mind for it is unlimited and accrue more power to you than you can possibly imagine.

Changes are caused and begin from the inside which is the subconscious mind.

THE SUBCONSCIOUS

Some of the most famous words ever written by a philosopher are "*I think therefore i am*" student of mind science like me would agree with Rene Descartes that without subconscious mind, there wouldn't be much left of us but only a body.

No sense of identity, no personality, no comprehension of THE past NOR THE future. The subconscious does trillion things right now just like killing of germs, fighting bacteria, regulating the flow of blood. The subconscious keeps you alive and at the same thing help you succeed.

As the conscious mind is knowing, self-assertive and has will and choice. The subconscious mind is the channel of all thoughts. The subconscious mind does not differentiate real from imagined. Its duty is actually to transform thoughts into things. It is a great servant that receives data from the conscious mind through all the senses and starts its transformation of bringing any information from the conscious to effective.

Subconscious mind unlike mirror molds the convictions of your thought, about your perception and cast them into reality. It is the field where ideas are planted and it harvest strategies to bring those ideas to accomplishment.

The mind is your most trusted friend, he who masters it becomes more like a master mind but he that fails to master it becomes enemy to self, and cannot believe in self, neither will anybody believe in him, he becomes victim to life's threats and blame the environment for these.

Understand your mind and understand self and accrue power to yourself than you could ever imagine.

MAINTAIN A MENTAL DISCIPLINE

"People like you more when you are positive for no one want to associate with the negative people, be the magnet the steel always want to cling to."

According to Kyle Xy, *"The food quenches hunger, water quenches thirst and positive thinking quenches obstacles."*

Success and happiness begins with a positive state of mind for good things begins with the right state of mind so keeping right is the first step to mental discipline.

Since we are aware that our thoughts hold the creative ability when right thought occupy the larger part of the subconscious mind to become the state of mind and put you to the right direction that has abundance in stock for you.

You will become unstoppable in that task you are in. people suddenly stopped executing the project that could have eradicate employment in the society because of continuous news by the media of a bad economy which set such people's mindset because they would start seeing reasons their plans can't thrive.

Every one of us is a self-fulfilling prophet and whatever we set in thought even in our closet even those secret thoughts of ours is influencing some things in the remotest part of the world, for you to maintain success and happiness then develop a character that filters out the penetration of negative thoughts.

We all know that Millions of ideas, images, and suggestions are constantly flooding into our subconscious mind through the conscious, it could be easy to reprogram yourself for success by disciplining your mental indulgences by neglecting any negative influx into the subconscious and feeding it with positive diet for a time being and see how your life will flee from limitation and blossom on beautiful life of success and happiness.

Constantly remind negative thought patterns that your mental house is occupied with positivity and buff up your vigilance and live a life worth living. Your mind is the central processing unit you either program it or leave the environment do it for you, set it to excellence or rather set it to failure all respond to the mindset you program.

A woman always come to work bubbling, basking in glory and lightening her countenance with smiles and she attracted promotion beyond her imagination and her colleague always appear very depressed has exhausted her query and WAITING TO BE LAYED OFF, the knowledge of this rescued her and brought her back to life.

When you feel depressed with negative thinking it affects your health and when your health is affected death follows. Job in the Holy book knew this and that was what saw him through HIS trials, David too know same.

People need a place to lean on therefore make yourself such a person by being positive at all times and see the brighter side of life. We seldom help anybody coming to us for assistance yet appear to be negative based on what they say, unleashing signals that they don't maintain a mental discipline.

The time to start maintaining mental discipline is now. Am not saying you should delve into anything you want without reasoning or knowledge of it and feeling like all is well. Get the knowledge of what you are doing but positive attitude to it makes you more effective and opens you up to a much better way of driving that thing higher.

LOW SELF-ESTEEM

No one likes to be with someone with low self-esteem because they make every moment boring. According to my observation no body have won any award by being low self-esteemed, awards are given to the bold who creep out of their shell to present their best which was good enough to earn them a prize. Low self-esteem means little or no self-love.

When we are not showcasing healthy, vibrant self-love, it becomes impossible to love and respect others or to love life itself. People who are in harmony with themselves in spirit, mind and body radiate positive self-love that saturate the entire place, they hijack every moment because they don't just live every moment they make it count.

Low self-esteem is a big social problem because it limits a person only to his comfort zone, even in the home such people show limited association.

Developing esteem entails drawing of energy from wonderful moments experienced. As a person motivates himself in needs to perform in the activities involving groups, such a person get embodied with new consequences which will motivate someone to act, in so doing eliminates low self-esteem.

The character to attract success and happiness doesn't work in accordance to low self-esteem. Low self-esteem is scared of what people will say and think, it thinks involvement is not worth taking any risk, it brings you down and leaves you with no comfort, and it is the enemy of our social environment.

Such people are limited, less effective because they have shot their doors to the world and crawl to self-judgment of the past, they are bringing in grenade from self and is blowing up their present and the future.

It is not the kind of life you would envisage. If you are a victim, it's time to start unlocking these chains that is tiring you down and start living because life is too short to be on the low side the rest of your life.

"*Just do it.*" is the NIKE's emblem and this book is now telling you to just do it without looking at faces at both direction laughing at you.

Get those new experiences of answering those questions in class, contributing your idea at the conference hall and let every new experience build in your memory a positive you with the mindset that no one can make you feel low except yourself.

BELIEF SYSTEM

"*Calling those things that be not as if they were.*"
"*If you want to change, first of all change your belief system.*"

Your belief is a guardian to your mind, it stands right in front of your mind and determines what goes in and what goes out it serves as your survival mechanism. Whatever you do not believe are not allowed into the mind and whatever you believe works for you.

The advertisers understand this concept that is why they show a superstar who enjoys a product and becomes great, they just need access to your belief and they prepare a concept to break the defenses your belief system might pose. But the truth is whatever you believe works for you because it entails programming your mind in some sort OF WAY and it works like that.

A pastor was travelling on a long journey and unknowingly he hit down an Hausa man although he sustained a slight injury but won't stand up, the pastor wanted to carry him to the health center around but he refused but was demanding for an injection then how can he receive the injection without a diagnosis if at all he needs injection and to know what injection is required but the Hausa man needs the injection instantly.

The pastor had to get a fresh and clean injection, then took some water into it and injected the man and behold he got up and moved away. What happened to him? You may ask but it was just his belief system at work.

OPEN TO NEW PERSPECTIVE

To unlock your hidden powers entails that you open up to new perspectives, when you open to new perspectives you become like the Japanese who get knowledge from all corners of the world to harmonize it with the ones they have INORDER TO BE more powerful. Change your belief and open to new things that will take you to great heights.

CHAPTER THREE
UPGRADE YOUR MIND

Your rising and falling all starts in the mind, you can walk the way of life and get high jacked by great tribulations and trials of all kinds but when you win your way through then will you realize that a test for gold is casting them into fire, when they are brought out you will see how bright they will shine. King Leonardis of the Greeks saw victory with his 300 armies against Ataxerves ruler of the known world as of that time.

When the Greek council refused to render him the Greek army because of their democratic practices, King Leonardis put together three hundred of his personal guards and armies to fight the greatest war of all time.

You can gather yourself and prepare your mind for greatness, success and happiness. But begin with a mental image of prosperity and success.

Whatever you visualize, you materialize. Karl Marx's mental construct was the brain beyond communism which was being popularized by Stalin of Russia. The world moves when you think and when you put in immeasurable actions you get the result. Keep up the good work but do your best with imagination.

UPGRADE YOUR IMAGINATION

If you can dream it, you can do it.

Pastor David Oyedepo ONCE wrote somewhere that "*Imagination is the pacesetter for your destination. It is the vital laws of the spirit.*" Imagination is boundless and limitless; it is a vision that tells where you're going.

Your imagination is the designer of your destiny. You can't imagine success and fail and vice versa but for no reason should you be caught dreaming of failure because your imagination is your creative ability, it is a reflection of what you can be, do and achieve.

Every man's rising and falling all starts in mind. Whatever thing you want to do in life is first of all imagined in your mind, it is image in action in the mind so let your mind's eye get to the destination to see how beautiful it is then work relentlessly and you will get there.

Imagination is the only map you have to that beautiful

and wonderful uncharted island you want to dwell in, get upgrading your imagination because there is no limit to what you can imagine.

You upgrade your imagination by thinking highly of yourself, by dreaming big and assuring yourself that you will get it beyond all odds. Don't forget that self believe is confidence; recognize that you are one of the powers on earth; your dreams make you so.

Believe so much in your dreams and in yourself and watch your imagination being upgraded. The earth turns on its orbit for us. Let me share with you one of The Secrets. The oceans ebb and flow for you. The birds sing for you. The sun rises and it sets for you. The stars come out for you. Every beautiful thing you see, every wondrous thing you experience, is all there, for you.

Take a look around. None of it can exist, without you. No matter who we thought you were, now is the time to know the Truth of Who you Really Are.

You are the master of the Universe. You are the heir to the kingdom. You are the perfection of Life. And now we've known this, meditate upon it and let its knowledge sharpen and upgrade your imagination;

making you to become invincible and unstoppable.

SELF TALK

Remember the words your mother told you WHEN you were young and still on her laps shaped who you are and formed your character, even now that haven't changed.

You can talk greatly to yourself, energize your mind with those great words of yours and see how great you become. Certain poems we recite when we were kids help program us towards what we will be.

RECREATE your mindset by saying positive things to yourself, talk constantly to yourself about the greatness ahead, convict yourself that you can and don't forget that you are the sum total of what you've heard since your birth, so this is the reason you should mind what you hear and what the friends you keep say to you.

If you have not heard that you are a genius why not convict yourself that you're one. Remember the greatest motivation that you hear loudly is the one you say to yourself.

You can be a self-fulfilling prophet if only you talk

greatly to yourself about how great you are. Learn to diffuse every word that you hear about yourself each day, take time to DUMP negative words INTO the cabbage and accept the positive ones. The negative words you DO NOT refuse will add up to who you are which is a sum total of what you've heard.

CREATE INTEREST

Before you succeed in anything you're venturing into, you must give your interest to it. That interest conditions your mind to take note of that thing you want to learn or want, it's time to debunk all negativity and start getting interested in that skill acquisition, that job and the course. Getting interested eases your mind to it which creates excitement to learn or perform that with ease.

WORLD OPPOSITE DAY

When you are charting that new project for human enjoyment, you will always get negative word or reaction from people, all you have to do is to make that day world opposite day, a day when every "*no*" you get means "*yes*" because on that day the world gives you the opposite of the real thing. Take there "*you can't*" to mean *"you can."*

Remember people who have dreams created everything around you. In our world when you are going after something big many people will tell you *"no,"* you can't and you won't.

The motivation to keep going must come from the *"Yes I can"* you tell yourself. As far as you know where you are going just go ahead and learn how to tell yourself *"yes"* because it is the immunization to that *"no"* that is meant to pull you down so when you're caught up with a *"no fever"* the *"yes"* you tell yourself is the only recommended pills for now.

As you keep talking to yourself based on the *"yes factor"* bear at heart that things don't always turn out as planned due to scarce values and resources and wrong strategies but that makes events more memorable and piles to your experience bank account to aid you become better next time.

CONCENTRATION

Successful men and women all need to cultivate the character of concentration. When you concentrate you get your mind to dwell on a particular thing at a given time, it makes you bring out your best to do that particular thing, get your mind focused on a thing and you will see that you have a mind that can do all things.

Enhance that ability to focus and dwell your mental energy on them and see how great you will become in whatever that is involved. Learn the act of concentration and get that goal achieved.

READ WIDE

"Readers are leaders." It doesn't matter how much of everything you know, what matters is how little of everything you know. In developing mentally you ought to know because you are what you know. So many suffer due to ignorance, when you know you attain another level of consciousness.

The most important thing about knowledge is that it makes you attractive; it helps you connect with people everywhere you go. When people realize how much you know and how much they can learn from you then will they certainly be loyal to you. People want to see how you can use what you know to help them, as long as you know, find time to teach others.

I will also like to share with you that what you read determines who you are; a sexual immoral person will always be seen with pornographic books and magazines, while a politician will be seen with newspapers and news magazines.

Great people are seen with great books. A way to found out more about a people is by going through the books in their library, smart phones and in their closest without oral findings about who they are.

Read wide but dwell greatly on the things that will aid you attain to your destination. Take time to read about those heroes you admire, most of us see our heroes, we would say *"one day I would be like them"* but it doesn't just end there, don't just cherish the moment, get to find out what they did to become great and you figure all these things only when you read about them. Keep reading.

CHAPTER FOUR

THE POWERHOUSE VIRUS

According to Robert Greene, the author of 48 Laws of Power; *"If you feel lost and confused, if you lose your sense of direction, if you cannot tell the difference between friend and foe, you have yourself to blame."*

Our greatest enemy is ourselves, because innate in us lies our emotion that produces virus that is deadly to our power house the mind. Those viruses could be fear, malice, anger, anxiety etc which terminates what we are working at, since good things begins with a right frame of mind fear retards your immune system, it affects your brain power, makes you lack concentration, fear makes you forget because it renders your brain blank. Fear and anxiety both produce similar responses to certain dangers.

But many experts believe that there is important demarcation between the two. We are no longer faced with the fear such as walking on the road and suddenly have to face with a lion or tigers. The kind of fear am talking about are the fear you confront whenever you start a new project, take on a new venture and fear of asking questions etc.

Fear is natural, successful people feel afraid but they understand that fear is something you naturally face on your way to greatness, but they tame theirs without letting it stop them and they walk along with it. They feel the fear and still do the work.

FEAR: A DREAM KILLER

Fear is false evidence appearing real! I traveled to my country home to see how my grandmother's domestic fowl was allowed to stroll far and wide to still locate back their home at the little cage built by my granny by 6 pm. This made me wonder and i began to ask questions of how she was able to tame them and why they will still come back freely, little did I know that my granny was able to do this by controlling the fowl's thinking.

When these fowls are being bought, a very strong rope is being tied around this fowl's leg and attached firmly around a heavy wood. As it face the challenges of pulling this heavy wood over a period of time it get familiar with the place in so doing will never forget this place till they stop existing even though it was fully capable of escaping. And we are like that too. Our thinking limits us, just as the fowls did usually due to fear.

The truth is fear can steal your dreams. You may be scared of rejection. You may be afraid to fail. If you give in to these thoughts and believe that you can't achieve your dream - You'll be right and therefore unable to achieve your dream.

Most times that we ARE AFRAID OF has no connection WITH reality. But as you read this topic about fear you will definitely find out that fear is not a monster in your closest but a thin air, all you need do is to open up the doors with faith and the wind of courage will blow fear away.

FEAR OF TAKING RISK

People whose country run a capitalist society are always scared to invest in the stock market, fearing recession, some are also scared of being capitalist by investing into business because they are afraid of losing their money. Successful people always have a clear vision of what they want to engage themselves into, then enquire more into it because information are the key component of a successful man.

Though what he wants to venture into may be the unknown to many who will criticize your new found task and tag it to be something no one had ever done before.

At times people see how so many people had failed in that same thing and advice you not to venture into it, all those *"don't,"* are you sure, what makes you think you can" creates fear but you don't have to compare yourself with anyone, you are a success and can make a different. The reason why it didn't work doesn't mean it won't work; it's just that the strategy towards it didn't work; a change of idea, concept and packaging can make it work.

FEAR OF "I MIGHT BE WRONG"

Fear makes your voice unheard; fear swallows the urge to make an attempt. IF you a graduate of a higher institution then you might have felt some kind of fear when the lecturer throws a question to the class, and a person rises up their hand to answer the question though you know the answer but you would never be the person to answer the question because of the fear of being wrong got you stocked on your seat.

Bringing it down to corporate office, some people are scared freak, to them everything goes, they don't contribute to opinions that contribute to the growth of the company or organization because of the fear of making silly statement, some are scared of challenging their boss even though the boss rides on them. Their boss who perceive their fear will play on them by turning them into slaves and watch them languish in penury.

FEAR OF THE FUTURE

In my sophomore in the university I got so much scared about the future because of my bad grades and it controlled my behavior and the way I react to words because when people talk about success I will only keep shut because I thought I was never successful. It affected my results the more.

This mentality changed my perception of the world. I spend more time mental envisaging what a heck my future would be. But the books and seminars I attended took away this mindset and set me on a mental diet of positive thinking which geared me to the successful man I am today.

FEAR MAKES YOU FEEL LOW

Fear makes you hate yourself; it makes you blame yourself in everything. Fear is first of all a killer of self; the worst thing a man can do to itself is to allow fear to weaken him mentally.

Fear makes a person feel less motivated and continuously make same mistakes. It blocks the mind from being motivated by packing racks of fear to make a trial. Fear leads to indecision in times of danger in so doing people have to make your decisions. Fear makes you a normal person instead of a creative person that you're.

HOW DO I CONQUER FEAR AND SUCCEED

According to Marianne Williamson, *"Your deepest fear is not that we are inadequate, your deepest fear is that we are powerful beyond measure."*

Fear is not only our biggest enemy but our constant companion, and we can overcome it. An author once wrote: *"Think of your comfort zone as a prison you live in--a largely self-created prison. It consists of a collection of "cant's, musts, must-not's,"* and other unfounded beliefs formed from all the negative thoughts and decisions you have accumulated and reinforced during your lifetime.

Fear is the evidence of what is real but might not be real because it is emotional. Every fear is like a bar in that prison.' But the good news is, because fears are feelings then you can choose how you feel.

Though Michael Ignatieff says: *"Living fearlessly is not the same thing as never being afraid. It's good to be afraid occasionally."* Fear is a great teacher. What's not good is living in fear and allowing fear to dictate your choices, allowing fear define who you are.

If you want to succeed then you must start standing up to fear, taking its measures by refusing to let it shape and define your life. How to succeed in place of fear is going for that *"yes"* you tell yourself and move forward to take that risk and not playing it safe, succeeding entails you going for the best while neglecting fear and its consequences, realizing that good things is yours for the taking but fear will always tell you it's not for you.

You don't overcome fear overnight but gradually, day by day, you can get it by the scruff of the neck and bring it under control. Instead of being afraid of taking positive steps to make yourself better rather be afraid of not having self-respect.

Be afraid of waking up one morning and asking yourself *"what did I do with my life."* Use this fear to inspire yourself to figure out what counts most in life. Then go get it. In so doing you are indirectly installing anti-virus that cannot deactivate or expire for a life time.

DOUBT

Doubt is your greatest enemy, and one funny thing is that you create this by yourself. People doubt for so many reasons and may be because of some negative attachments to your perceived past may assume doubt about the future, people take time to scrutinize in their minds to see if there is any past occurrences and if any there will be disbelief whether the current things we want to embark on will be workable or not, some people's doubt emanates from their ego while some emanate from as an information being delivered by a source you thought is unworthy and you begin to doubt.

Self-doubt is more dangerous, It affects the way you perceive the world, it limits you and SHUTS you out of the world and out the real people who will help your dreams come true.

Obinanju Catherine Udeh popularly known as Dj switch emerged the first winner of the world's biggest singing reality TV show, X-factor in West Africa. She is a young woman who has done things her own way and still loves to do it her own way standing completely and absolutely by the values she believe in.

She enthused about her professional dreams, projecting among other things that boundless optimism and belief in herself became the necessary amours against the daunting blows of fate.

Such buoyancy and depth no doubt are resultant from the rich medley of her enviable background, education, exposure and open mindedness and curiosity.

She never doubted herself, she never doubted that she would win the competition. Utmost believe is faith and it is the opposite of doubt. Negative belief can breed doubts but positive believes do rejuvenate us and help us get more information about what we want to attempt.

This information will empower us and such empowerments is anti-doubt syndrome. When the information is clear, we now have a clear knowledge of the stuff and the enablement is guaranteed hence leaving no chance for doubt to steal our dreams, opportunities, hope and vision.

FAILURE

Failure has a way of making us feel inadequate and incapable of trying again. When failure takes its place in our mind it makes us weak and discouraged. Failure makes us feel unworthy when it takes its turn on us. We settle for less because we think we can't attain certain height; it stops us from fighting and slows us down in grabbing opportunities. Failure breeds fear that makes us think that we are unlovable and to hate everything that surrounds us, most of us have succeeded in linking fear into our values as human.

Most successful people failed many times in the respective part of their life but still succeed and their stories are not far away. Don't you think life would be boring without failure because when you fail you not only count what you loose but also count the experiences gain.

Never forget that a thing doesn't work doesn't mean that it won't work but depends on the concept and packaging but when it fail it means that there are some things that you need to get right.

See failure as an opportunity to learn not an indication of your inadequacy. It is high time we changed our concept of failure, let's learn from it.

Get to free your soul from the chains of past failures, and live the present with love and worthy to try again as Thomas Edison, Walt Disney and P.T Barnum and still counting; I encourage you to start seeing failure as a step forward.

SELF-PITY

Self-pity cannot allow you to change your reality; it is a prerequisite to failure. Self-pity can be found in pretty much all of our lives, some people seem to pity their lives and dwell on it for long instead of figuring out a way to move forward.

Self-pity sometimes comes when we feel that we were treated unfairly and later we will compare ourselves with others. The danger of self-pity is that it causes us to believe that somehow we deserve better than we get, it has its bedrock on selfishness.

Self-pity tries to remove us from the realities of life by believing that only good things should always be ours and when things don't go as expected we tend to pity ourselves.

Life is a game of interest and interest sometimes clash so know that being good at all things doesn't mean that people will treat you fairly. Self-pity is rooted in pride it, we battle self-pity not because we feel worthless but because at all times we feel that we deserve praise for such reasons we tend to be self-centered and seek glory all times and if someone else take this glory, we tend to become jealous.

The solution to self-pity is being humble and do things not for glory but because the people deserve better. Take joy in seeing people smile and always do things to make people happy and not just to take the glory in so doing you are indirectly installing anti-virus that cannot deactivate or expire for a life time.

CHAPTER FIVE
WILL POWER

According to Emenike Odinaka, "*The body must obey the will, hunger and thirst are your greatest enemy, even the blood that flows through your vein, they must be mastered in other to bring your desired goal.*"

Let your will push you to the limit that will get you close to your aim even if hunger and thirst tend to stop you, you can always conquer. The movie "*Odysseus*" showed how "*will*" can go in getting you what you want.

After a battle in Troy he had to spend ten years traveling before he could return home. He was persistence to get home, resisting even the goddess who promised him eternity if he would stay with her and give up going home but he believed that he will get home to see his wife and kid and though all odds became against his goals but his Will to get his aim helped him get home to his family.

Raise above what any other person wanted, set the standards to the extent that it will propel you into action not just action but enough action that spell satisfaction.

Let your willpower make you grow above material things which is natural to the ordinary man. When you unlock your will power and become aware of its wonders you will harness its beauty to become extra-ordinary, remember that challenges and obstacles are the ghost that comes with holocaust because of probably clash of interest, scarce resources and discouragements but never it elude your memory that real men don't compete only kids do, just believe and your *Will* will trigger of to pilot your body to get all your desires.

Set your pace not based on competition but based on limitless possibilities which is the brain behind leading personalities, companies and cooperation. See for instance *Chiwetel Ejiofor* is a British born Nigerian whose parents came down to Lagos Nigeria for a wedding ceremony but on their way back to their house in Lagos they had an accident and Chiwetel's father died and he sustained a lot of injuries but all these didn't deter him from pursing his dreams.

His first movie was with Steven Spielberg's and he was part of the movie *"2012"* which had grossed up to $700 million with Chiwetel winning several awards. He is an officer of the Order of the British (*OBD*) when people complain that blacks scarcely made it to Hollywood he fought to become the few.

Let this mindset unlock your Willpower to know today that you can always beat the reach, top the list and champion that vision to reality. But you need a goal to work with for that destination you want to reach.

This is the power to will and act, for us to unlock this great power then we need to put some work on the table and iron them out. Life seems difficult to people who lack the technical know-how of life.

Little do most of us know that life is like mathematical BODMAS has its own formula. And if such formulas are clearly followed, we will understand the things we need to know which makes success easy. Though it may require patience because of individual differences and man's inability to see the world the way you see it, these might cause a lot of them not to attend to us when we need their consent.

BE A MAN ON PURPOSE

Channel your purpose to be a problem solver, design your purpose in a way that it helps people discover themselves. *Asa Candler*, the known founder of Coca-Cola wanted people to feel a thirst of something different from Bailey, Champagne and spirit. He wants people to drink something that will serve a dual purpose which are: refreshment drink and medicinal purpose.

This reason brought out other major players who have other dreams for themselves but was channeled towards making Cocoa-Cola a world brand.

Be a man of purpose and you discover how to get life to dance your tune. Your life is tied to your purpose stake your life to it, if you fail your future will be ruined and don't think you have anything to fall back to, work furiously to GET it .you cannot fail

GET A REASON THAT STIRS YOUR SOUL

You are your own worst enemy. You waste precious time dreaming of the future instead of engaging in the present, since nothing seems urgent to you, you are only half involved in what you do.

The only way to change is through action and outside pressure. Put yourself in situations where you have too much at stake to waste time or resources - if you cannot afford to lose, you won't. Cut your ties to the past; enter unknown territory where you must depend on your wits and energy to see through. Place yourself on *"death ground,"* where your back is against the wall and you have to fight like hell to get out alive. - Robert Greene author of 33 Strategies of War.

Most times we would have vision and dreams but we never had reasons that is stirring our soul, think of the movie *"Superman"* Clark Kent knew he had powers but always had reasons to act, tell yourself that you are the only person with such dreams and just like Jesus your purpose will help solve the world problems and how immediate you are determines the number of lives, marriages, structures, organizations and truths you will save if not executed in time.

Most of us lock up ourselves in the comfort zone of self or probably are still enjoying what our parents kept for us without going all out to make the world a better place for human, trees and animals alike.

LAW OF MOTION

"People who say it cannot be done should not intrerrupt those who are doing." - Chinese proverb

The more the increase in resistance the greater your potential.

Newton's third law of motion states that *"for every force, there is an equal, opposing force."* It's the same here- no big dreams ever come true without an equivalent form of resistance, the bigger the resistance, the greater your potential to attain your dreams.

The biggest achievers in the world got to where they are today only after overcoming endless resistance. Whenever I face a roadblock, it tells me *"this is something worth going for and I definitely jump it over."*

The more roadblocks in the roads of life as we jump over them the better we become. It gives a better version of what I hold in my mind when I overcome these blocks and achieve my goals.

"Obstacles are there to prevent you from getting to the other side." The above quote clearly shows what is at that other side. Which means they are where dreams, goals are. Goals are the reason we face challenges, and that obstacles are clearly presence in whatever goal you're working towards, they stand to make that goal unachievable but without these obstacles it will only be

a child's play and won't be valued by no man or woman.

Obstacles like walls stand our way and it just mean that you need to push down walls to get to where you're going. See the challenges as the only the test to weed out people who don't believe in your dream and limits too much competition because will power defers and yours is the highest so keep going.

Sydney Smith saw obstacles as those frightful things you see when you take your eyes off your goals. Spending more time staring at your obstacles are like packing crisis into the mind, instead spend more time thinking more on the challenges and there solutions, stay strong because if you don't face anything, how then can you call yourself a fighter?

GOAL ATTAINMENT

"If you want to be happy, set a goal that commands your thoughts; liberates your energy and inspires your hope." - Anonymous.

It takes only you to know where you're going. Being aware of the reason you're on earth underscores clarity of where you're going to, it becomes the magic that turns ladders into elevators. Your utmost desire to achieve greatness will spur you in setting goals that measures out ways of which your aims can be attained.

It have been proved beyond measures that the brain is a goal attainment machine, its mechanism is based on the instructions given to it by the sub-conscious mind which is always in control.

THINK IT OUT; WRITE IT DOWN

It all begins by thinking, whatever you think out be sure to put it down. Ink what you think inside your sub-conscious mind, let it sink inside there and aid in bringing those things you desire. There is really power in writing your goals down.

WORK TOWARDS YOUR GOAL

Can anything stop you from pursing your goal? The answer is *"not at all."* May be conditions are stirring at your face, finances seems to be running and your love broke your heart. All these things HAPPEN SO AS TO SCARE you out from working towards your goals, remember what you are about to do will change your life and the world in general. Are people telling you that it is unobtainable like they told Edison in his bulb experiment yet he succeeded?

People don't want to hear how many ugly situation and challenges you encountered that made you fail, all they want to hear is that you conquered and brought back shining gold the way Chris Air had it all rough but still possess a jewelry company. But the good news is 21st century leave clue as guidance to your goal attainment.

Get some facts on how your role models made it and advance from there because there is nothing new on the earth surface, all you need do is an improvement of what is already in existence in a much better way.

ACCESS YOUR EFFORTS TOWARDS YOUR GOAL

Though the road might be filled with block blocks like the Nigerian highway but I believe you can still maneuver. Access your efforts so far to know whether to increase your efforts or to still operate at same pace. At times accessing your efforts makes you ascertain whether you're still on track or have strolled away.

LEARN FROM YOUR MISTAKES

Hard work and learning from mistakes. Despite what some people say, you never get anywhere without hard and whilst we all make mistakes; the even bigger error is not learning from them (*Ladi Delano British/Nigerian entrepreneur the C.E.O of Bakrie Delano Africa, 31 years old as of 2013*)

There is an old saying that says "*Show me a man who has never failed and I'll show you a man who has never succeeded.*" Though you may study the profile and biographies of successful men and women but that won't stop you from making mistakes because mistakes are inevitable in life.

After you might have accessed your efforts towards achieving your goal, highlight your mistakes and don't let them ruin your goal.

CHAPTER SIX

EMOTIONAL INTELLIGENCE

According to Dale Carnegie, a pioneer in public speaking and personality development, *"When dealing with people, remember that you are not dealing with creatures of logic, but creature of emotion."*

Your mind is your almighty intelligence, it have capacity to function on its own. It would be very important we know that human are creatures of emotion. And as we develop our emotional intelligence which will influence character in return and as you carry on with it, your success and happiness will be inevitable.

Emotions give meaning to life and to us, to the people around us and determine the way we relate to even the people we don't know.

This emotion is so powerful that it forms the foundation through which we understand ourselves and relate to others, when you become aware of your emotions thoughts no longer flow thro an fro your mind because just like reflex action your emotions act as signals to what you are thinking at a point in time.

Emotional intelligence can help you bring clarity to thinking and enhance your creative thinking, it can help you be in control over situation, aid you in stress management, enables us deal more creatively and actively with people, it also enhances boldness, helps you trust and introduce empathy in your dealing with people.

WHAT THEN IS EMOTIONAL INTELLIGENCE?

Emotional intelligence is the calling up our awareness on how we and others feel, why we feel that way, and the knowledge of what can be done about it. It is the ability to comprehend and utilize the power of emotions with wisdom.

Mahoney and Salovey defines emotional intelligence as the ability to monitor one's own and others' emotions, to discriminate among them, and use the information to guide one's thinking and actions.

It is not enough to know that the emotion projects our feelings we also need to come to the knowledge and value them in ourselves and in others, respond appropriately and to apply the information effectively.

LOSING CONTROL OF EMOTION

Whether we are aware of our emotions or not they lie inside of us and for the people that are aware of it are enjoying a life worth living and are influencing things around them. We often say what differentiates us from other animals is that we are rational and can think but this is partially true, we can cry, laugh and show some emotional range.

We rationally plan out our day and that make us pretty much in control of our daily routine but in the presence of adversity we reflect a confused, fearful and impatience side of us and when an enemy, colleague or unpredicted friend attack us our rationality dismisses then we will feel a sense of betrayal, bitterness.

We can now see how emotions are influencing the things we do in every moment in every way. But bringing how we feel under controls elevates us and makes us high minds and capable of influencing things and matters because we no longer react but instead we respond to them with intelligence.

Losing control of your emotion will result to so many things which will include making you behave insanely and these occurs when you either get angry or in a rage, sexually aroused, when you feel fury which is often categorized as losing your temperance.

Losing control emotionally could also make one to live in isolation. A man lost his mom he loves so much and he suddenly loose control of his emotions, he cried and stayed indoor for days without seeing anyone.

A woman who lost her temper when she had a misunderstanding with her husband, she comes to her place of work and wouldn't work effectively and efficiently and a company where her services is greatly needed would have a deffect because of her lack of ability to handle her emotions.

Emotions influences a lot in our lives and wouldn't be handled with lavity. We need to be emotionally intelligent.

Be in control of your emotion and you start improving your communication skills, take your relationship to the next level with the power not far away but inside your own emotions, unlock it by just being aware of it and using it often and on but positively.

MODEL OF EMOTIONAL INTELLIGENCE

Daniel Goleman's emotional intelligence model, figured out four primary elements of emotional intelligence of which he comfortable separated into two, Personal competence (*Internal*) and Social Competence (*External*).

PERSONAL COMPETENCE (*Internal*)

Which constitute the Self-Awareness: this is actually being aware of your thoughts and feelings; it is the coming to the knowledge of yourself. That is having a deep understanding of one's emotions, as well as one's strengths and limitations, values and motivations.

It further helps you recognize who you are; what you like; help you communicate clearly and effectively, it help you get motivated and act clearly and often times help you make strategic decisions, get that goal and help you build sound relationships etc. in these personal competence is another model to aid proper understanding of ourselves.

Self-Management: when you manage your behaviors and mind the choices about your actions. From self-awareness flows self-management. It is the choices we make to respond to our emotions. Self-management is like an inner conversation that keeps us from being locked up in the prisons of our emotions.

SOCIAL COMPETENCE (*External*)

Social Awareness: this involves having empathy towards others, which is actually putting yourself in people shoes. Being aware of other's needs, wants, expectations and emotions are otherwise known as empathy.

Of all the elements of emotional intelligence, social awareness is most easily recognized in others. It is not just taking actions to try to please everyone, but rather understanding other people's feelings and perspectives.

Relationship Management: this entails relating with others and managing the relationship you create, this is where self-management and social awareness come to play.

Here we find the most visible tools of personal leadership: persuasion, conflict management and collaboration. Successful relationships boil down to managing others' emotions effectively.

EMPATHY IS YOUR EMOTIONAL RADAR

According to Carl Jung, a Swiss psychiatrist, *"There can be no transforming of darkness into light and of apathy into movement without emotion."*

Empathy is a word being cut out from sympathy but meant quite different thing from it. Empathy entail you view things from another person's perspective, to inquire about their perspective and not assume they see the world as you do, everyone have their side of a story and this skill is immensely important to successful relationship both with coleagues, classmates, spouse.

This important emotional skill makes us effective and efficient, it aid the brain in the right task to perform. It makes us harness cause and effect from other perspective as regards their own side of the story and not just claiming that other people view the world the same we do.

EMOTIONAL BANK ACCOUNTS

You can buy people's time, you can buy their physical presence at a given place; you can buy a measured number of muscular motions per hour. But you cannot

buy enthusiasm... You cannot buy loyalty. You cannot buy the devotions of their hearts. This you must earn.
- Clarence Francis

In real life we have banks where we deposit and make withdrawals, such is true with our emotions; we deposit and make withdrawals of emotions. The relationships with other people are all about emotional bank accounts----ours and that of those people that we are in relationship with and this is also true for the people we make contact with every day of our life.

Remember we give life to the world and loneliness can kill, this is the reason we need to learn how to relate with others to foster proper relationship. Your emotional bank account reflects the sum of deposits and withdrawals that you have had with a person over the course of the relationship.

Deposits represent the positive things that you have done or said to build a supportive and trusting relationship that has trust and respect.

No matter how weary it seems keep it positive by complimenting others, being supportive at the point of need, apologize when you're wrong and be appreciative at all times to make deposits always. Don't make negative or abusive words on others because it is bound to CAUSE A withdrawal.

I met a salesperson in a fitness shop down the road who complained immensely about how his boss insults him and wouldn't care about his welfare. How would this man possibly respect the boss or even BE devoted to his work? All this are question we ask when it comes to emotional bank account.

Most times people you're good with and have contributed to largess in their emotional bank account may tend to get us pissed, bear in mind that they might have witnessed a lot of withdrawals that day, instead OF PICKING UP A FIGHT you can make use of that opportunity to deposit more to put a smile on their faces.

When we find ourselves in any relationship we have automatically open an emotional bank account; all negative words and deeds are making withdrawals while positive words and deeds make deposits.

Always make deposits all the thing and flee making withdrawals with abuses, curse, ill-treats, and malice.

Most times the big quarrel didn't start at that point in time, you might have made withdrawals from time to time and without any deposit, when there is non left it leads to an outburst.

It will also be true that in life people alone don't make withdrawal: situations, conditions, challenges, obstacles and hold ups on our roads can cause a withdrawals too but instead of allow them make the withdrawals learn to see the positive in all of them and you automatically recycled it to make deposits.

But there are people who are naturally bad, they tend to look for troubles, they insult, abuse, they also see the bad in you. Its certain they are withdrawal from you all the time; instead of waste time with them just allow them be. But all the time make deposits.

TAKE CHARGE OF YOUR EMOTIONAL BANK ACCOUNT

Never forget that your niceness towards people won't stop them from making withdrawals by the day in our emotional bank account. WE should take charge of our emotions just as no one has the right to make withdrawal from our bank account without our permission so is true with your emotions too.

When you take charge of your emotional bank account you will come to the full knowledge of how you feel at any given time and know that it is your choice to feel bad when people make withdrawals no matter who they are even your closest friend or family member or even your greatest enemy.

Time is too short to spend some on bad feelings when it can be channeled for more productive purpose that will transform your world positively.

Remember before any withdrawals would be allowed, you must append your signature first; most times we append these signatures without much thoughts, we blast, shout, abuse, curse without knowing that bad step can be taken back but negative words can never be taken back.

Take charge, think before you speak, don't sign for withdrawals by replying negatively to someone; everyone has his or her moment; he or she simply had a bad day just helped him or her to regain consciousness by creatively responding to them and not reacting to what he or she said or did.

LAW OF PROFIT

This book is committed to help you build all round relationship that will enhance your prosperity and happiness. Man is a creature of profit, add commercial profit to everything they do.

Before any man could render extra service to you then you need to pay for it either monetarily, emotional or in kind. When you plant a seed of corn, you get a comb of corn with countless seeds meaning that naturally we are creatures of profit and nature made it so.

God in his infinite mercy made man in His image and likeness to prove that He is also a creature of profit he presented His only begotten son to save the whole world to himself. Isn't it profitable? By nature we are born to make gain in anything we involve ourselves in and that's the motivation behind every business.

Learn how to use them and see how simple life will be even in school. The law entails that a man cannot go into something without seeing his profit or benefit clearly. This same law is what the European Leagues are using. European players are better than their counterparts in Americans, Africans and the Asians but because they give commercial value to their leagues, which attracts the best players to ply their trade in Europe.

So make a nice offer that people can't reject, at least give them something to benefit in whatever thing you are involving people into, no matter who they are and they will join you to it.

WITH CLOSE RELATIVES

If you really want acceptance, love, warm welcome and even better money from close relatives then don't visit them empty handed especially when they have kids.

You must be ready to add value everywhere you go, it must be in cash or in kind or even be a source were they derive maximum happiness which is depositing into their emotional bank account. Also make a mark each time you are around your relations, get the kids their favorite candies and cartoon Videos, help them get home works done. On their parent's side, remember they have needs and is seriously looking for someone to fill them, let that someone be you.

Sometimes they will need someone to trust, someone to share their deepest secrets, to care, to laugh with, someone to advise them, make them trust you to this.

Firstly, while coming get something no matter how small it is, or how rich they are they will value your gift, if they have kids show these kids love and their parents will trust you.

Help with the house chores; just make your presence felt. Add value to that home, find ways to reduce their cost and they will do anything in their capacity to pay back and also beg you to return next time. Also learn to say thank you and be cheerful always, it add to their emotional bank account.

Learn to make impressions every now and then by calling your loved ones from time to time and not just when you need their help.

WITH INVESTORS OR PARTNERS

This law is also potent when you are seeking for people to invest into your idea or vision, you ought to show them how they will gain from that vision before they invest their time, energy and money to your vision.

Be committed to help them achieve theirs in so doing your vision is becoming a reality. People don't just join you they join you because through joining you they will get something out of your vision that will change their lives too.

People need to be making profit to enable them develop the world we are living in. it is the desire to make profit that drives our world, get that fact right and sideline your own gains out of the plans while presenting it to a client or an investor all that you should focus on is how they will profit out of your vision and they will love to do business with you. Make life a *"win-win"* game and not a zero sum game and enjoy a smooth ride to success.

WITH EMPLOYER

According to King Solomon, the wisest King that ever lived, *"A gift of a man makes a way for him."*

Human want all their efforts rewarded and forget that sometimes you don't always get all your benefits due to the fact that you don't know that you need to win your bosses mind to yourself, let this law play its part by getting your boss a gift of something he wouldn't resist.

Don't focus on his huge salary he takes home but focusing on your task ahead which is winning their heart to yourself. Don't blame him for his harsh nature, he is just being insecure and must build wall to protect him or herself; if you were in his or her shoes you will do the same.

Robert Greene in his book 48 laws of power wrote that when you give your boss a gift you become equal with them. You will gain there heart in return and they will shower you with favor. Also Robert Greene explained better that you deposit to their emotional bank account by letting your boss know that you are loyal to them, don't speak ill about them, don't act like you know so much, do more and talk less.

You only break the spell when you say it before doing it, enjoy the surprise in their eyes by doing than talking. A junior pastor never got promoted over a year and he was worried about this while other pastors who he came before got promoted. He became curious and always receive the same answers when he approached the senior pastor who tell him to keep working hard which he is sure of doing. Until he learnt the secrets hidden in this book, he realized that the senior pastor's wife has influence on HER husband then he targeted the woman who he showered her with gifts and within a short period he got the promotion.

So what are you waiting for? Know that all humans are born to MAKE profit so try any positive means to create yourself in people's mind by unlocking your hidden powers and acknowledging that all human being are not just emotional and rational creatures but also creatures of profit because their rationality other than emotions make them so and your use of this knowledge will gain you access to their emotions which is the key spot. Use this to your advantage to prosper and build an outstanding relationship with people.

WITH YOUR LECTURERS

Love your lecturers course, be passionate about it and let them know, go to their office to learn more but female students should also be careful of male lecturers for they are humans and not trees; then offer yourself to help them arrange the books or scripts on their table, for the female students it will be adviced you again to became mindful of the way you deal with male lecturers.

But most of the lecturers yearn for your company. Relate well with them, stand out in various assignments, read more before going to their office, answer questions in their class and they will beam their attention on you, go for extra lessons in their office but don't appear too needy, don't fake it though, You will be a friend and he will fight for you in point of need.

FLAUNT YOUR STYLE

Successful people are people of style, they live with style because to them success is a lifestyle that guarantees well living. As you go further in life learn to be a person of style, a person who is tipping in a restaurant, bar, or in shopping mall, a person who is appreciating a good thing when you see it.

I went to a cafeteria with my best friend; I called on the waiter who responded with need to serve me and my friend. To her greatest surprise I offered her some cash to take care of me and my friend. Amazingly she cheerfully met our needs with hesitation. Running errand for us wholeheartedly without even minding the next person. This is paying people to give you extra treatment.

Another occurrence is going to the fuel station, walked straight to their supermarket bought three loaves of bread then gave the SALES girl who sold the fuel one, she was SURPRISED AND since then I became HER special friend and whenever I come to buy fuel and had to queue, I SEE HER FEELING DISTURBED AND always wanting to help OUT. That's the power you radiate when you learn to flaunt your style. It saves your time and energy and also makes you influential.

LAW OF RECIPROCITY

This law is as potent as the law of gravity which makes any heavy object you throw up come down without hesitation. Law of reciprocity looks similar to the law of profit but law of reciprocity is more practical, it is more like the golden rule of what you sow, you reap even more.

This law tells us that you get even double of what you give out may be not necessarily from the same person but you will surely get it back. With this law you will even find out that when you greet someone, they will even respond twice the greeting. Try to be that person that when you face challenges, people get busy just to see a way to help.

Be that person that people are always pleased to have the OPPORTUNITY to repay FOR all the kindness, care and support you'd shown them over time. Nature doesn't always give you back that love from where you gave it.

Your generosity to one person may be returned by a complete stranger. But if you keep putting it out wherever it's most needed, you'll keep getting it back in buckets.

I've made a move to further the level of which I show care to all the people I love and the people I didn't know, and am sure to be getting it back in folds from even people I don't know. It's by putting other people before yourself that you get the most out of life. By helping other people you help yourself.

While I was serving in the Nigerian Youth Corp, a passing out Corper called Prince Ice left his belongings and promising another incoming Corper to possess; he told me that this incoming Corper may not know this arrangement but he deserve it, nature had prepare it already for him through Prince Ice and behold the young man who inherited those belongings didn't say otherwise; I saw the way he was being favoured from all angle.

He sowed somewhere and he is reaping some other places. Isn't life interesting? And there are many more ways only if you know about the favor factor.

CHAPTER SEVEN
FAVOUR FACTOR

According to Ben Franklin, *"Diligence is the mother of good luck."*

People are given birth with a sign of favor on their face, instead, favored people are, without realizing it, using four basic principles to create good fortune in their lives. Understand the principles and you understand favor itself more importantly, these principles can be used to enhance the amount of favor that you experience in your life*

Overtime scientist have studied many things but rather neglected the favor factor probably because they think it can't be empirically studied but we begin to wonder why some people had success carrier while some didn't; why some tend to have a nice day while others hadn't; why some people have a fulfilling relationship with their spouse while others hadn't; why Some people even with low qualification can get the nicest offer? Studying these occurrences we will categories these set of people as favored people and people who hadn't these chances are classified as people without favor.

Being a FAVOURED PERSON goes beyond winning the lottery and the raffle draw. Though when favor is mentioned our thought ARE CHANNELED TO religious folks, but know that you can create your own favor by making the right choices.

MAKE THE RIGHT CHOICE

A favored person knows that his decision shapes his reality. He is more rational knowing the wrong choices is an economic waste on time, money and resource then they decide to makes the right choices either.

A man of favor believes that satisfaction is putting enough action, he works hard to really research and brainstorm in any decision he is going to take, and he scales his decisions based on the most advantaged and less disadvantaged and vice versa, comes out with the best choices with the greatest possible outcome.

A FAVOURED person knows that the world is filled with people with some imperfection and understands that there will be clash of interest and works against this.

Favored people are not fast to jump into a glaring good offer, because they understand that everything has a price tag. They take time to begin with where it ends with the mind to iron its challenges in due course and prepare for their occurrences.

Being at the right place at the right time is an attribute OF being favored, BUT WAS CREATED BY THE RIGHT CHOICES MADE and are maximized by those who use their intuition.

INNER SATELITE / INNER RADAR SYSTEM

Intuition is a sudden flash, an internal knowing a glimpse or vision of truth, sensation that runs through our body telling us that something is or isn't right even though our rationale may suggest otherwise. Your inner guidance is continually scanning your inner and outer environments, sending back messages. Your intuition informs you of what is taking place and enables you to instantly make sense of the huge amount of information that continually flows within and around you.

Intuition is a way of accessing the inherent power of your brain. Your consciousness only uses a tiny proportion of your intuition access the residual power and communicates to your consciousness the bank of wisdom and knowledge it has available. This is done subtly through thoughts, feelings, sensations, images, sounds or any combination of them.

People of favor master their mind through meditation or contemplative thought. They connect to the Infinite intelligence who speaks to them anytime, anyway through their conscience that never lies and is being transmitted through dreams or that little voice that you hear when danger want to set in.

People are tagged unlucky when stock market crashes and their business dwindle while some people advance in whatever they do. The favored people understand that the unconscious mind does most of the work in their body and also attract whatever that dwell in it for long. They trust their intuition when it speaks to them.

Accessing your intuition helps you make the right decisions; it could be practical way to produce sensible and reliable information that helps you in decision making.

It gives immediate access to options that rest outside of the confines of rational thought. It would be important we use our intuition in walking through life so that with its knowledge and ability we can instantly draw into its limitless source of guidance and wisdom. They have the answers to most perplexing questions and receive clarity about any issue or situation.

Ben Carson got this sudden flash in a dream that helped him had the answers of his final medical examinations that seemed like hell to others before the exam. It's so pathetic to know that only very few in our world uses this great power so.

DEVELOP YOUR INTUITION

"Everything else may leave you; money, power, people but your shadow will not leave you; why is it so? It is your support team; your closest friend. Believe me."

All of us inherently possess this great software that scan, access, and articulate issue that we are facing. Many stroll around with this software with no knowledge of how to use it; this innate ability aid in rediscovering lost memories, clarifies the unknown or predict outcomes.

Each person's intuition is unique and remains personal to them, though people are using their intuition but need to be conscious about this great guidance system. Being aware of its techniques and how you had used it opens the door of developing it.

For example it was its power that you were able to know that a gift was right for someone, it was its power that interpreted to you that you left the house without taking with you something important like your keys, files, document, mobile phone, biro or maybe laptops.

I believe that every single one of us has intuitive abilities that work the way you use your muscle. If you don't use yours, then it becomes weak. So like any muscle the more you use it, the stronger it gets.

There are people who receive thought waves from the air, become such people by Simply developing your intuition through constant meditation and let your mind remember the dreams you had because there are no such thing like a dreamless night.

That dream might be your intuition showing you the way ahead. Since this is a day you had never seen before tune in with your intuition to live every moment as if you had lived it before.

If you are thinking about someone and they call you, then you are in contact with the intuition at that moment. Another way of developing your intuition is by believing and having a conscious awareness that you have a metaphysical support team behind you.

This support team guides you and teaches you. You have to be in good relationships with this team, interacting with them, most people go in the mirror and speak at it; to them it is their closest friend. Become conscious of it and then converse with it.

A woman suddenly became restless and had feelings beyond her rational reasoning, in a short time her cell phone rang and it was a report about her husband and the accident at the mine where he works.

SO EMOTIONS FLOW WITH THE INTUITION AND TELEPATHY REALLY OCCURS, SO WORK ON YOUR INTUITIONS.

AURA: BROADCASTER

People get favored with this because favor has its bedrock on your aura. Our being is more than just our physical body; we have a complex energy system, which is our aura that serves as our energy channels. An aura is simply an extension of you, categorized as your self-concept.

You higher aura depict your state of mind at any moment while your lower aura depict your state of heath. Your state of mind influences your state of health. When your aura is strong it propels you and makes you be at your best every moment in happiness and influencing things.

But when fragile or damaged it can make you drained, unwell and feeling disconnected from yourself. Think of your aura as your self-image, a covering like a giant bubble that simply flicks off in any stressful, disturbing and discomfortable moments.

When fully charged it makes you be in your best and sharpens your power to influence. Although everything has aura both plants, animals and human being but the aura of humans are quite different from that of the inanimate objects.

Our aura as human changes in response to our health and our emotional level at a given time. Human being are intimately yoked to the environment and we respond viscerally to circumstance and people around us, Probably if a place tends to drain your aura due to the manner of the people or how the environment looks like, it is likely you will like to move away from there.

This is because of lack of equilibrium between the two auras. Your aura at its best will automatically influence people and make them like you, and if your aura is low it makes you less attractive and pleasing to people.

I was at a meeting with my fellow colleagues when a beautiful girl came in though she had an aura of some sort but another girl who is not as beautiful as the other came in participated fully, filled the whole room with humor. She took everyone's attention and they wish she would stay forever. That is aura that is fully charged.

Discover yours and learn how to use it for an effective you. It can earn you respect because your aura gives you style and attitude which interprets respects when well managed.

A damaged aura can be healed by draining energy from a healthier aura. A fearless man can make a fearful loose its fear and start feeling fearlessly. A RICH man already has a rich state of mind and CAN GO AS FAR

AS GETTING SOME MONEY FROM THE BANK WITHOUT ANY SHAME, AS THE BANK will be willing to give but A poor man can't do such.

A rich aura is bold, filled with confident and can even drain other people's aura, that is, your aura getting to subdue OTHER peoples, that is making people leave their way to do some things for you.

Imagine Aliko Dangote coming to your house, naturally you will go out of your way to make him comfortable not because of his name but because of his aura.

Your lifestyle, character, personality and emotional state are subtotal of what makes up your aura and the psychic center channels energy to all these. I have a friend whose aura is fully charged that he call himself Fearless which he was, my association with him took my fears away and I became as fearless as HE WAS.

What kind of aura would you like to have, is it an aura of your boss or that of a king which draws people to you and make you favored everyone you go then the good news is that you can develop it and if you already had it then you can build in more to it. Because an aura is built every day of your life.

To develop a highly favored aura then you must bear at heart that you don't just wake up the next day with such aura. To develop an incredible aura, an aura that will make people fellow you even if you're not a footballer or even a musician, then the first thing to do is to start being positive.

Learn to remove most words that limit you, words like: *I can't, what if, I don't think it will work, it won't work, I'm afraid* and *no*. Your brain like A computer can be reprogrammed to function the way you want them to if you eliminate the negative words and start *"positive words"* installation that will help you shot down the stars.

Learn to say it is possible, I will, yes, I can, absolutely, definitely, I do, I believe. These words when constantly channeled to the subconscious programs it And will reflect a positive self-image.

People are looking for a source of energy, wouldn't you be a source that keep peoples hopes alive and give them power to keep moving in life.

There are five things that help build an incredible aura that in turn create the favor factor:

Burning Desire, Belief, Enthusiasm, Self-Image and Communication

BURNING DESIRE: This entails a desire to transform to a better you. How much do you want this power to influence and become powerful? It is not necessarily determined by how rich you are. Your burning desire can spur you to change from how you are NOW to a new form embodied with charisma, a clearly defined personality. This propelling force will help you.

BELIEF: As small as these concept is, it is the reason why we fail or succeed. Our belief system contributes to who we are. It is necessary in aura development. Belief that nothing is impossible and it becomes. What are you afraid of? You need to know that fear is just a false evidence appearing real. Believing in your positive statements strengthens your will power to act.

ENTHUSIASM: This is a feeling you can't buy in a shopping mall, you can't fake it and you can't borrow it. It is being propelled from zeal to progress a vision. Your enthusiasm builds your confidence and sustains your aura. If you don't feel enthusiasm in any stage of your life, ranging from getting a spouse for yourself, or progressing a project, pursuing a career or whatever, just stop for a while and ask yourself "*what*", "*why*" "*how*". "*What*" will entail you redefine your purpose, "why" is asking for your motive, remember motivation is motive plus action, get the "*why*" and the "how" will take care of itself.

This will automatically positive affect enthusiasm which triggers your aura to bring you the favor you want.

ATTITUDE AND SELF-IMAGE: A man went for an interview, ON GETTING TO THE FRONT OF THE INTERVIEWERS HE WAS SENT OUT. He felt confused AND PONDERED ON a lot of unanswered question.

Little did he know that self-image is very important He complained of spending years in school without being taught self- image. Little did he know that he is to develop these by himself. Some of the identifying characteristics of a poor self-image are lack of self-belief, a poor attitude which drains self-confidence an important energy to power the aura.

Not having a target breeds low self-esteem in us. Be a man of purpose, inquiry about the field you're going into and you will be an expert at it and you will agree

102

with me that knowledge is a potential power; it makes you confident of yourself which creates your attitude and sharpens self-image.

Since the way you dress determines the way you are addressed and the way you are perceived determined the way you are received. Clearly defined aura makes you presentable. A favored fellow sharpens themselves by looking good and talk soundly.

I read about a cashier in a bank who imitates THE dressing STYLE and TALKS like the manager while others talked casually. In less than a year the young wan became the branch manager while the other cashiers said he was just favored without realizing his underground efforts.

Though it is good to be yourself but change is the only constant thing as far as it keeps favoring you. A favor factor entails you taking enough action before you win praises, it will make you cut down on many bad habits and so many things to earn you what you want.

Though at the onset it might seem like you're not being yourself but constant practice of being what you want will become a part of you and you will forget those days of practice. Our body and mind stretches like elastic and takes a new form of what we practice constantly within three days.

COMMUNICATION: Your ability to convey a message orally to another person with clarity requires your self-image. You need to work on your communication and also learn how to be empathetic. It can go to chapter five of this masterpiece and find out more.

NETWORKING

Though favor can be a good thing happening to you by chance, favored people know that this kind of favor can be manufactured and no wonder they go out day by day without adding one or two phone and email to their contact, in fact to them meeting people is a hobby. Favored people make new and quality friends and allies because to them meeting people increases their chances of having a positive encounter.

Since favor entails good thing happening by chance, they open doors of new chances everyday by meeting new people every day. Jack Canfield helped Stevie Eller who fell down and had a nasty cut on the leg. Just for this good gesture Stevie got him nominated for membership in the academy which earned him a Golden plate Award, joining previous recipients such as U.S former President Bill Clinton, Placido Domingo, George Lucas, New York Mayor Rudolph Giuliani, U.S Senator John Mc Cain to mention only but a few but he got this award through helping a person he never knew before.

Each person you meet might be a life changing tool or probably provide you a better job, may lead you to BETTER opportunities or even new ideas to run that business, you can even meet your life-time partner, you can get great sponsors for that business that you think isn't going to succeed.

If you are really going to classify yourself as a favored person, then start up a good conversation with people while standing on a queue for a bus, train or A.T.M because whether consciously or not the greater the number of the effective contacts you have the greater your chances of getting favored.

I boarded a bus and met a graduate of Quantity survey who just finished a Masters Program. He got favored to participate in building a new University just because he started up a conversation with a man sitting next to him.

Go ahead and meet someone today, if you're scared get freed with the knowledge that everything in life is a risk, even if your smile wasn't returned, you must learn to say "*A next TIME*" because meeting him or her will add to your chances but if they reject your regards or shun you remember your value is still intact until you let it dwindle.

Learn to deal with rejection by shapely moving to the next person; with your ideas in mind you are selling yourself to greatness. Learn how to start up a conversation, remember people are most times insecure and scared. They learn to trust you with time per positive words you say, be humorous and kind and scan the people you meet; make sure they are worth your time.

THE "NEXT" GAME

Learn the fun in the "*next*" games; say next until you win your contact of the day because all you want is to create more chances for a positive outcome and your heart is not transparent for people to see the purpose for the spontaneous discussion so they might misunderstand you so understand them and try the next person. For students in the high institution you're given that freedom to meet as much people as possible to aid your chances of being successful and that is the reason behind changing rooms every session.

Meeting people might entail boldness but don't be arrogant. Since human loves themselves and would like to be appreciated, then why not start be appreciating whatever that is worth appreciating after all that's the reason they spend time stirring at the mirror.

You even acknowledge their brilliancy or good attitude so far in that function or ceremony; go ahead to ask for the brain behind what they do and start up a discussion about their varieties of stuffs in your mind probably clothing labels, learn about their dreams and how the world would benefit from it.

Start with little things first like fashion, artiste, music then advance to enquire about their purpose in life but level your conversation according to their age but don't forget to be empathetic (*read empathy in page for more insights*).

HELP PEOPLE

A favored person recognizes that everyone is born for greatness. He helps people attain their positive height. Favored people don't fancy "*I don't give a damn*" attitude. They inspire, motivate and encourage people get to any height they desire. They help people on the ladder freely hoping that on helping people he is helping himself.

He desires to help people who sincerely needs help because he knows that sometimes it's not about the money but a word or two, even an idea, a little suggestion, and comments, giving out new ways of doing things. Or do you think such things don't count? Your wise words can go a long way because those words of yours can encourage the channeling of a million dollar to SOLVE ONE OF THE world's biggest problem.

ATTITUDE TOWARDS WORK

If what is worth doing is worth doing well then if you are sweeping the street do it well because favored people know that there are radar beaming on them and that their reward aren't far away.

I usually buy things in a shopping mall, and today seems to be that special day when I met this salesperson who took all the blames thrown at her by customers, she apologized with respect and not like other salespeople who would rather snub customers and clearly SAY in their minds; their mall is flooded with people so whoever is not satisfied with their services can go.

Sometimes I feel unhappy buying things there but they enjoy the monopoly. It would be better to buy things on high rate and go with your emotions intact than being punched by a wreck less shop keeper who doesn't care about your feeling, but on that faithful day instead of meeting the saucy shopkeepers, I saw another well-kept GIRL whom I thought was new to the shop.

She treated people with respect, listened to people's complains and took the blame. She appreciated her customers, also she recommended the best products and also wearing a warming smile that radiate the building, she is humorous and relieves people's pain.

Who won't like such a wonderful gal? Everyone queued to her side all the time and the other sales girls felt jealous of her. I enjoyed the queue because it gave me an opportunity to meet WITH new people and take home new contacts.

After a while I recommended my friend to her, he checked on her and saw how she got along with people and made her an offer to employ her with a salary that was triple what she earned with free accommodation.

Aren't she favored? That's what a good attitude towards work brings. She never knew me but I saw her good works and it was pleasant, I never had a choice than to make sure she's rewarded

TAKE CHARGE

Favored people believe they are in control always and because they are in control they expect the best because they believe that when they expect the best they get it. People who classify themselves as favored always get what they want from life because they took charge.

When you take charge that means taking responsibility of what happens to you. Favored people accept feedbacks and are not at the mercy of mere events, they don't just work hard but rather they also work smart.

They are relaxed and are more likely to see opportunities than THE UNFAVOURED PEOPLE WHO WORRY A LOT. Favored people see what is there, rather than trying to find what they want to see.

They accept that openness to new perspectives and experiences takes them out of mental slavery with the mindset that "*doing the same thing persistently will always lead to the same result, they better learn new ways of doing the same thing which opens the doors of opportunities which increases the chances of positive outcome which the end result will in turn favor them in the long run.*"

Favored people enter a race because they can. They take charge and work diligently to attain their SET goals. They create chances and when the possibilities seems slim they open up another door with their favored character.

SELF FULFILLING PROPHET

I've always believed in magic when I wasn't doing anything in this town. I'd go up every night sit on Mulholland Drive, look out at the city, stretch out my arms, and say *"Everybody wants to work with me, I'm really good actor. I have all kinds of great movie offers."* I'd just repeat things over and over literally convincing myself that I had a couple of movies lined up. I'd drive down that hill, ready to take the world on, going, *"movie offers are out there for me, I just don't hear them yet."* It was like total affirmation antidotes to the stuff that stems from my family background (*JIM CAVEY-actor*).

Don't forget that you are a prophet yourself; whatever you say concerning yourself will definitely come to fulfillment.

If you want to stretch your comfort zone then bombard your subconscious mind with prophesy on big bank account, a trim and healthy body, exciting work, interesting friends, memorable vacations- of all your goals are already complete.

The technique you use to get all these are by prophesying these things to yourself. On prophesying these things to yourself you are sending message through your subconscious mind to the infinite intelligence who start working out plans to bring those things to you.

Clement Stone does this, Napoleon Hill used this same technique. It worked wonders for Andrew Carnegie.

Why not make positive prophecy on yourself using present tense and see how favored you will appear in people's eyes.

RECYCLE ALL TO YOUR ADVANTAGE

All things works together for good for those who are favored. The fiancé of Roland a friend of mine had an accident which lead to the amputation of her two legs. I told him not to worry and his response was that he is favored.

I was surprise at his response but he further said that some people round the world would've been glad to step into his shoe but did not because they lost their loved ones but he is favored having to feel her hands on him. I learnt this lesson from Roland and I had to share it with you to.

There are people who wish that they are in that condition you're in now. You are simply favored to be able to breathe the everyday air and to see the rain fall on you and the snowflakes descend on you.

No matter what the situation is, no matter what is being said to you bear in mind that they can be recycled to your advantage if only you don't resort to self-pity. Seligman called it "*explanatory style*" in his book "*Learned Optimism*" which explains away misfortune so that it is not indicative of a whole person's being.

Favored people experience bad times but they never dwell on them rather they focus on what can be learned from that and in so doing seize the opportunity that drives by.

They see benefits not the ill-fortune. They believe they are in control of their life and everything that happens is for their best interest instead of asking why and tagging themselves as unlucky.

They see the job seize as an opportunity to get a better one, they see the world as an open door and when one door closes another opens, they believe that a finish line is a beginning of a new race, they know that a race track is circumnavigating and you stop when you want to.

They see jilt as a good thing because to them people who can't make it with them on life's race should crash out of the race rather than pulling them backwards in life's race and at last stopping them from fulfilling life's purposes. Now you don't have a choice than to take the lead.

CHAPTER EIGHT
TAKE THE LEAD

The warm bath of nice scent, the fanciful clock sitting on its soft shadows, the wonder chair on which I sat and the immortal voice of Michael Jackson were all good but letting you know that a leader lies in you is much more better, as these upsurge heated in my heart I then stood to look out through the window to notice an impressive array of richly blooming rosebushes lined at the drive way, there heady scent filled my nostrils and I prompted to think that if this moment was used in obsession the implication will cost the world something great, there should be a change and you would rather be the change you want to see was what Mahatma Gandhi said, I then took charge, took my biro to write you on taking the lead, by taking the lead, you make head way. What matters is that you are a light and lights shine for people to see.

People sit down and make criticism about bad leadership but yet fail to even participate in the leadership process. Some won't even like to be good followers; they tend to be less concern in matters concerning the well-being of humanity in there vicinity.

It's high time we start knowing that leadership is not a one man thing, it should be collective. The moment we start being conscious of the world we are into and the importance of passing a better world to the upcoming generation, then will we see the need of being proactive.

Every individual should know that you should not leave this world the same way or even worse the way you see it, let us strive to make our respective society a better place for human, animal and plants. We usually think leaders are majorly organizational head, committee heads, institutional leaders, chancellors and vice chancellors, principal to mention only but a few.

It would be necessary we know that everybody, boy and girl, men and women, old and young, big and small are all leaders in their own respective way and forms.

DEVELOP YOUR LEADERSHIP TRAIT
Although natural gift differs from one individual to another but the ability to lead is a collection of skills almost all can be learned and improved upon, this

process of learning and improvement doesn't just a take a day.

Leadership is complex and highly encompassing, it is multi facets. Taking the lead makes you hunger and thirst for respect and this is built by developing these leadership traits. It is high time you have to come to the awareness that you are a leader because everybody is.

Being conscious of these reality is a great step to the acquisition of the leadership trait because it takes you a higher step above the crowd. People tend to acquire this leadership trait while being in position of leadership which is not supposed to be.

America is termed the world best not just because the territory are lucky or that the land is fertile above all other but because large number of people started seeing themselves as leaders of not just of American but of the world.

The world best attached to them is a function of enough individuals thinking the same way. To develop the leadership trait then you must strive to know, leaders are curious people and just need a grasp of the facts. Without knowledge you cannot become a leader.

People believe you based on what you know. Every other person is subject to him and dependent on him based on the knowledge at his disposal. People fellow you because you know much more than them and that knowledge makes you the center of everything.

If the difference between ordinary and extra-ordinary is just that extra then why not get extra information to get taller. Associate your mind with greater mind on the pages of books. On getting informed you will research more on your field of focus but don't hesitate to know little of everything. In taking the lead, don't just be satisfied by being mere good be excellent, discover what it takes to be great.

VISION

You have to dream and for the dreams to come into reality you must forecast the future. For you to take the lead then you must make out time to think more often.

It is only vision that set the pace for your destination, until you can see where you are going to and how to get there no one would be able to follow you because vision is one of the major factors in taking the lead, without vision we will have nothing to stay ahead with, vision entails seeing things and people not the way they appear but the way they could be.

For you to make head way then you ought to have a vision. A leader must be zealous to see farther than other people's eye could see. When a leader stirs at the sky, mind you he must be seeing the Saturn ring, when he look at the floor he sees the underground waters and when he looks at you he see a star who is meant to shine.

Remember Edison saw a light bulb in the midst of darkness; Martin Luther King Junior had a dream. Remember Walt Disney once had a vision of the Disney World and Henry Ford once had dream of building a petrol-driven car that have to sell in the market for multitudes to buy.

Leaders know that at time the things that are real are not the things every eye can see, like the water flowing underground filling our creeks and rivers, like the wind we can't see but feel it as it caress our body. Like the electric current that flows through wires.

Leaders see beyond the surface, they wield the ability to see a CEO in a pauper, they see a forest in a seed. Their thoughts are not rigid they make it flexible and enjoy its benefits.

SEEK KNOWLEDGE

On taking the lead opinions and wishes are eliminated for facts and figures. I can remember a saying that says *"if you're not informed then you will be deformed."*

The average zone is never your platform, get information because it is a driver to your vision, it delivers details to your vision and empowers the mind, no matter how swift and clear your vision, you need information to speed up the process, information brings every vision into accomplishment, it makes vision effective and if you want to take the lead then you need to get informed. Getting informed gives you the opportunity to rub minds together with the great and sound minds in the leaves of a books.

LEARN TO FEEL IMPORTANT

For you to take the lead then perform with pride that which you are called to do, regardless of its title, position or profession. Imbibe into yourself a humble pride in whatever thing you do, that's the only way people can see the importance and seriousness you attach to what you are taking the lead for.

Get excited about your vision on being glad about what you are leading, make people want to reckon with you. You are what you think so therefore what you make of yourself is what people will take you for.

Billionaires are perhaps more aware that most of the best things in life are free, if the most things that are considered a necessity like air are free and you can acquire it then let this be the best reason to fill important.

EMOTIONAL STRENGTH

Dr. E. Doyle McCarthy (*1989*) puts it, that emotion is a fundamental social category, a mould for our mental lives. Emotions themselves are objects we handle and seek in the contemporary drama of self, emotions are internal figures that play out their lives in the theatres of our body, though we are creatures of emotions but to take the lead then we should be emotionally strong.

Emotional strength makes you capable of not acting sometimes in the face of danger, because waiting deliberately at times presents eventually opportunities you had not imagined. Being objective enough to minimize illusion are the key of all timer.

Remember Solomon the wisest king said there is time for everything. In taking the lead, you must acknowledge that self-deception can cost you your vision, know when you are flattered and don't let pride take you on when you are praised, remain positive in face of adversity, building your mind to be stronger than your emotions.

STRATEGIES OF TAKING THE LEAD

In becoming the great leader that you desire, bear in mind that little things count, greatness can begin with mastering and working out these practical strategies.

FAITH

We can paralyze the hands of marauders of day and night and every militating force against us, we can rescue supernaturally every kind of disaster be it on the air, sea or land. Beside we have the authority to change the law of nature if only we obtain faith.

Faith is dead to doubts, dumb to discouragement, blind to impossibilities, knows nothing but success, faith lifts its hands up through threatening clouds and the rumbles becomes gone, taps current from the Master Mind who has power on heaven and on earth, who makes it flow just because of faith.

Dr. Roymond Edman made a statement that faith makes the up look good, the outlook bright, the in look favorable and the future glorious. Faith makes you receive a vision, believe it and give you the ability to work it out.

Abraham a nomad became the father of nations; Judah the intercessor became a Royal line; David the shepherd boy became a king; Joseph the prisoner became a prime minister; Esther the orphan became a Queen; Deborah a housewife became a judge.

All these are as a result of faith exhibited that transformed vision into a reality. For you to take the lead make faith a paramount thing. Faith means seeing it before having it, it is the assurance, the joy in your heart of having what is hoped for. Great man had done great things through faith. Do not stop believing said Prince Ice.

PREDETERMINE A COURSE OF ACTION

Another important strategy of leadership is to predetermine your course of action and allow these actions to unfold slowly then speeding them up at the right moment according to the tempt that you control.

Don't always be in a rush to believe just anything because people have a way of manufacturing something that looks like saint and faith out of nothing, take your time to evaluate people's suggestions before acting but if you are unsure of a course of action do not attempt because your doubts and hesitations will infect your execution.

LAY OUT YOUR GOALS

Taking the Lead requires that you become a goal getter that finally results to your transforming into a great thinker and great reader.

As an effective leader thinks out their goals, then writes them out before enacting efforts towards their goals. It will gladden my mind if you also know that mistakes are inevitable.

Great leaders learn from these mistakes. Don't relent; keep fighting, moving and working towards your goal. Leaders with a goal will definitely succeed. At the course of laid out goals you need a specific plan to execute. You need a plan that will stir your soul, be sure to work on them gradually

BOLDNESS

As a leader you need connections, as a leader your followers are looking at you for actions. You need to go out for it without minding what your pocket says. Don't base your boldness on how much you have either. Let it flow from within.

Timidity is dangerous when it comes to taking the lead, it would be better to appear bold to execute your vision, don't worry about mistakes you commit through audacity because they will be corrected by another audacity.

Everyone admires the bold, no one honors the timid, and it only sends the bad signal that you are incompetent. Send a signal that you worth a king's ransom even those who turn you down will respect you for your confidence. What would you loose by being bold and that respect you gain will eventually pay off in ways you cannot imagine. This is the David and Goliath strategy.

In a dignified way go after the highest person in the building because by choosing great opponent you create the appearance of greatness, boldness is indeed a strategy of a leader.

ALLOW TIME FOR ACCEPTANCE

Time is an artificial concept that we ourselves have created to make the limitedness of eternity and the universe more bearable and more human. Sure, we have constructed the concept of time; we are also able to mold it.

To some degree allow time for acceptances although time and people change, let us examine a few of the oppressive realities that endure and the opportunities for power they provide, change is slow and gradual.

It requires hard work, a bit of favor, a fair amount of self-sacrifice and a lot of patience, a sudden transformation in a given time will bring a total change, work with people, with utmost honesty and sincerity within a given time they will get to like your personality and the idea you are trying to project and they will be loyal to you.

EXPECT PROBLEMS

Being a leader is strategic because you make yourself powerful by being in the centre of events. The more you are in contact with others the more graceful and at ease you become but never forget human are social creatures by nature and power depend on your social interaction and circulation.

But be certain that there will also be problems from human and nature in general, since you're not running at the same time and the same program with others, there will certainly be problems because man is selfish in nature and individual interest might come to play. But a great leader with his wisdom and understanding will OVERCOME them all.

As a matter of fact a leader is not meant to please everyone, for you to satisfy the majority there will still be few others who won't be satisfied but pleasing the greatest number should give you the greatest joy.

FORSAKE ISOLATION

Always stand on the things that are right, but as you toll the road of life as a leader isolation shouldn't be a choice to make because isolation exposes you to more danger than it protects you from it.

Isolation cuts you off from getting the valuable information needed in pursuing a vision. Isolation makes you conspicuous, vulnerable and an easy target but things will go well enough when you are circulated among people. Make allies because when you mingle amongst people they become your shield in trouble times and get you the help most needed at a particular moment. Isolation will always create more problems. In that crew you formed lies a person who hold the highest sway who will motivate others to get the work done.

DISTINGUISH THE ASSET AND LIABILITIES

In your quest for good leadership, that will entail you have members but instead of move with crowds in which many breeds of opponent, suckers and victims exist. The highest form of the art of leadership is your ability to distinguish the wolves from the lambs, the foxes from the haves, the hawks from the vultures and this is the process of separating your asset from your liabilities.

If you make these distinctions well, you will succeed without needing to coerce anyone too much. But if you deal blindly with whoever that crosses your path then you will have a life of constant sorrow.

Leaders keep acquaints of weak men but don't disclose their schedules to them rather spend much time with their assets. It could be a selection of few men to work with, Jesus did this, Moses carried out this in the wilderness, Gideon did the same, Leonardis of the Spartan also knew this. It is just a selection of men and women who will help in bringing that vision to reality, who will motivate you and won't desert you.

You will have to invest more in them, make sure there are no liabilities because liabilities lack the right ideas and also lack the strategy to bring these ideas to work and they can also appear to be overactive to be noticed, oversensitive to draw the latest information and will proclaim how your plans can't cross the rooftop, some of them appear proud and are difficult to relate with because they are insecure and had build shields of PRIDE to protect themselves.

Know the men of ideas and action in one; men of ideas only and also men of action. Distinguish between these men and women and learn how to use them to accomplish your mission.

MISSIONS

A leader knew that every is bringing his dreams into attainment, so therefore they make every day their mission. They learn to divide their vision into missions and gear to accomplish them by the day. Don't be like Tom Cruz, make your missions possible and not impossible.

EMPIRICAL REQUIREMENTS OF A LEADER.

There are things needed in that CV of yours before you can mount the mantle of leadership Leaders gear to stand out, as a leader there are some requirement expected of you which are named and discussed below

INTEGRITY

On taking the lead integrity is inevitable, integrity means that you cannot be bought with anything at all, you must possess dynamic opinions and will, you must be bigger than a vocation to the most beautiful cities of the world.

You must not stand to lose your personality in the crowd but stand up to protect it at all cost. In taking the lead you must not stand to compromised with evil, you must not build your ambition based on selfish desires.

You must be a man of your words and must not do things because others did it. Men of integrity are not pushed by anger, they are not destructive, and they are straight forward in adversity and in prosperity.

These set of people do not believe that cunning and shrewdness is the best way to succeed, things must follow procedures or even due process. They pay homage to principles which form their guide. They appear real with no trace of THE superficial, they are not afraid of the truth when not popular. They design their course of action and remain true at all times.

If integrity seem hard to practice then you need more time to prepare to take the lead. Majority of the people taking the lead are people who fall into leadership by cruel means they lack character and integrity, they appear to be over zealous and ambitious but with little or no knowledge of what it takes to lead.

They are organizational illiterates with poor quality character and emerge as leaders based on their own selfish reasons. They are neither born nor nurtured with leadership skills. They appear as national emancipators taking the lead to end up learning to lead. It would be better you read this topic again to digest what it takes to take the lead. Integrity will brighten your countenance and help in your sociability.

SOCIABILITY : CREATING RELATIONSHIPS.

A leader will always answer the question. "*Who do you know*" what makes you a leader is that you must have followers, and that always requires the development of relationships, the deeper the relationships, the stronger the potential for leadership.

Each time I enter a new leadership position I will immediately start building relationships. Build enough relationships with the right people and you will be able to captivate the mind of your followers.

In relating with people a leader must understand individual differences and a leader must not personalize his or her member on course of relating with them, you are only to impersonalize your spouse at home and no one else, this also enhances your experience.

EXPERIENCE: WHERE THEY'VE BEEN

The greater the challenges you've faced in the past create a track record for you, these shouldn't be a discouragement for starters, as you keep moving build an experience bank and it will spur your followers to likely give you a chance to lead.

Experiences doesn't guarantee credibility, rather it encourages people to give you a chance to prove that you are capable. Nothing speaks to followers like good past records of integrity, an integral person will always be given a chance.

Personally there was a time I had a few challenges as a leader, I had to stretch myself to get the work done, I brought some of my experiences forward and my followers had a good reason to believe in me. It's not a must for conditions to be the same, situations are unique per time but your past experience will kill the fear and create in you a Will to try and your experiences will project our ability.

ABILITY – WHAT CAN YOU DO?

The bottom line for followers to queue around you is there knowledge of what their leader is capable of. That's the reason people will listen to you and acknowledge you as their leader. As soon as they can no longer believe you then forget it. The most important thing is your ability to deliver. People will believe in you because of your capabilities to serve them better. Learn what works and how to make them work, a leader is ever strategizing and your abilities will build trust.

TRUST

This is bedrock of every leader. You must live an exemplary life. A leader is a model the follower imitates and must be a character oriented person. This leader must be competent and connected if really he wants to be trusted.

CHARACTER; WHO ARE YOU?

True leadership begins with the inner person. That is why someone like Billy Graham is able to draw more followers to himself, because people has seen the deepness of his character

CHARACTER DETERMINES POTENTIAL

With character a leader can accrue some amount of respect; trust from his follower just like John Morley observed *"No man can climb out beyond the limitations of his own character."* This statement is so glaring when it comes to leading people. To back this up, let us take a look at Craig Weatherup statement which goes: *"You don't build trust by talking about it. You build it by achieving results, always with integrity and in a manner that shows real personal regard for people."* A leader with strong character releases an essential potential to lead.

CHARACTER A FLIGHT TO RESPECT.

According to John Maxwell, if you don't have strength within, you can't earn respect without. And respect is actually a necessity when it comes to leadership, leaders earn respect by making sound decisions that are applaud able, and all this decision boils down to the capacity of the character the leader possess. A leader knows that mistake is inevitable so when he makes one, he admits it instead of finding excuses and all these brings trust, respect and reliance.

Every leader is human and as humans we all have interest but when a leader puts his or her interest aside and is gunning for the interest of their followers then will respect be attributed to him or her.

TYPES OF LEADERS

John Maxwell; a leadership guru, a major tutor and writer on leadership taught on two types of leaders. These are the: positional leader and the real leader.

POSITIONAL LEADER: Positional leader is a leader in position; he is the person everyone is seeing as the leader. He is the figure head. He is aware of the power in his disposal. He gives instructions to his follower who obeys him but a positional leader draws must of his inspiration from the real leader. He needs to consults the real leader. He needs the real leader to help him in influencing decision. Am not saying they lack leadership skill but they possess little power of influence.

REAL LEADERS: This set of leaders speak later, they only need their own influence to get the work done.

These leaders can influence the whole house. The real leader holds the power, not just the position. They don't need to be in position to get things done. Today BILL Graham with his charisma is a real leader. His advice has been needed by world leaders especially the American Presidents. They seek his consent and his wise counsel. If you notice a disparity between who is leading the meeting and who is leading the people, then the person running the meeting is not the real leader.

Most times the real leaders are not in power but people give them utmost respect and the people's perception about depict authority. He is not in power but he has authority and whatever he says counts and most times when there are options people will be waiting for his choice for them to take side.

I encourage you to know the type of leader you belong and be sincere about it. If you are a positional leader then discover the real leaders among your followers and build allies with them so that you too can influence him to help in influencing the people. Every organization, in every member lies a real leader when you also unlock your behavioural Power.

CHAPTER NINE
BEHAVIORAL POWER

According to Aristotle, a Greek writer and philosopher, *"A good style must, first of all, be clear. It must ....be appropriate."*

In the field of psychology, behavioral science plays an important role. Aspects of style have been described by observers of behavior throughout history; however, it wasn't until the 1950s and 1960s that this area of psychology developed sophisticated theories.

Behaviorists simply watch people and describe their actions without any attempt to analyze why the person is behaving in a certain way. Included in this group is the well-known behaviorist, B.F. Skinner. Style behavior and social styles concepts developed out of this branch of psychology.

In 1966, David W. Merrill, an industrial psychologist, undertook research to explore ways to predict success in selling and management careers using a strictly empirical approach. He started with one basic truth: people tend to consistently behave in ways others can see and hear, and the words used to describe this behavior can be agreed upon by others who have seen and heard the same thing.

All people exhibit patterns of behaviors, we can achieve more satisfactory relationships. We can, in fact, increase our chances of success in any idea of endeavor where the "people factor" is involved- without needing a deep understanding of peoples' inner selves. Behaviours are projected by different styles we humans exhibit in our day to day lives.

If behavior what we say (*verbal*) and do (*non-verbal*). Then we also possess Interpersonal behaviors which is what we do when interacting with one or more people. Since human behaviors varies, we can't explain human behaviour without relating it to human styles. Because styles explains the variation in behavior.

WHERE DID YOUR STYLE COME FROM?

If several of your friends or colleagues were to follow you around for a couple of days and record how you behaved, you will really exhibit a wide range of different behaviors. Next, they would notice that you tend to use some behaviors more than others; some a lot more. Why do you suppose this is the case? Simply put, you use some behaviors more than others because they are the ones which make you most comfortable in relating to people.

These behaviors became comfortable for you early in your life. As you used them more often, they became your behavioral habits which is just your style. TRACOM's social style model is an easy-to-use tool for learning about your behavioral preferences.

It will help you understand why you find some relationships more productive than others. It will help you develop insight about your behavioral strength and behavioral weaknesses. It will help you develop a way of communicating with others, knowing that behavioral style is not good or bad, just different.

The model stresses the value of diversity as a way to build on your strengths and the strength of others to develop productive relationships in school, offices, at home and in the field. You socialize with this bahavioral style and that makes social style possible.

SOCIAL STYLE

Social style is a particular pattern of actions that others can observe and agree upon for describing one's behavior. And there are four social style. These analysis will project each style and translate on how to build on it to create efficiency and enhance your all round effective.

"ANALYTICAL STYLE"

ASK-TELL BEHAVIOUR

People of this nature exhibit a self-description that translate asking more than they tell. This is made possible because they sometimes delay participation until they get to hold a justifiable information. The withhold any form of action until a detailed knowledge about the subject at is at their disposal. They take time to be sure of their stand and this is more important to them than getting off to a fast start.

COMTROL-EMOTE BEHAVIOUR

These set of people describe themselves as being less emoting and more controlling. They perceive themselves as being under control and fact-oriented.

These set of people are comfortable in conditions where the task is the point of focus. They don't require a great deal of personal interaction. To them precaution is a necessity in carrying out a conscientious work effort and they take honor in keeping to a schedule and course of action.

GETTING THE JOB DONE

You are plan cautious and well organized in thought, you want to feel well balanced before venturing into any course of action, and most times your behavior is an asset to a cooperative effort with others. Taking time to avoid the potential for error and wasted energy is the way you like to still continue with a job, and others always look up to you.

Most times people may seek your counsel with regard to an in-depth analysis of a situation. In working with others, your tension level will be raised when they rush into action without thinking things out.

It will challenge you to be work with others most especially when there is an urgent demand for commitment to decisions made with very little information at your disposal.

At this point You will be uncomfortable because you are now focusing on the feelings other people project in the course of carrying out the work than dealing with the work itself.

You can appear overly cautious to many people and may be reluctant to take initiative or declare your point of view. Other people may become frustrated by what they view as indecisiveness on your part.

You can appear to intent on reviewing all the alternatives to a decision that you may postpone a decision longer than others feel is desirable.

BUILDING ON YOUR ASSETS

You can be very helpful by providing a stabilizing influence. Keeping your eye on the problem when others are impulsively jumping to solutions is an example of this.

In serving this role, be sure to appreciate the creative effort of others, even if off target at the moment. Others will possibly come to expect you to have details on hand. Expect this and come prepared to supply information. Be willing to share what information you have, even if in your own mind it is incomplete.

You can maintain credibility by expressing your discomfort and making your tentative conclusions available. A better relationship with others may be obtained by letting some of your feelings show in your everyday reactions.

SOCIAL STYLE-PERCEPTION "DRIVING STYLE"

ASK-TELL BEHAVIOUR

Your self-description indicates that you see yourself as more telling and less asking. This involves your being quick to interact with others, eager to get your ideas on the table, and energetic in the action you take with them. You see yourself as forceful in your relationships with others, willing to deal with competition and steadfast in the positions you take.

CONTROL-EMOTR BEHAVIOUR

You describe yourself as being less emoting and more controlling. You also see yourself as disciplined in the time you spend working with others and deliberately businesslike. You are independent, controlled, reserved, and task oriented as you are. You see yourself as factual, stern, and straightforward. You tend to avoid emotional involve with others, particularly in business settings.

GETTING THE JOB DONE

When working with others to complete a task, you see yourself taking the lead to establish direction and pace. Your attention to the task frequently places you in control of the situation.

You see that your willingness to make decisions is accepted by others who fall in line with your approach. You may take the *"I'd rather do it myself"* approach in completing a task instead of waiting until someone else is willing to take responsibility to get a job done.

You are likely to experience tension when others reach what you see as a timely course of action is subjected to endless debate and detailed analysis. Individuals may irritate you when they do not take a serious approach to the achievement of the objectives you have established. At times people might see you as telling others what to do, without listening to their points of view. This can make it difficult for you are willing to run over them in an impatient drive for results. You may also come across as arbitrary and critical.

BUILD ON YOUR ASSESTS

You can be very effective with others by properly using your telling behavior. Others may wait for you to express yourself so they can take the lead from you. Be sure you have your thoughts collected. Also, your directive style can help others keep their focus. So, find the best manner for expressing yourself and be a pacesetter. Your manner must not create interpersonal tension which will cause others to spend their energy resisting you instead of supporting a goal achievement.

To improve inter personal effectiveness; accept the value of others' opinions. Discipline yourself to listen to the ideas expressed by others even when the ideas seem to be based on subjective feelings. Be sure to really hear what they say-don't just listen to know when they are through talking; incorporate the data they provide into mutual problem-solving. Accommodate your pace to the slower pace of others make them more comfortable and gain their voluntary cooperation.

SOCIAL STYLE-PERCEPTION *"EXPRESSIVE STYLE"*

ASK-TELL BEHAVIOUR

Your self-description indicates that you see yourself as more telling and less asking. This will result in your having a tendency to interact with others in a spontaneous manner. This interpersonal behavior can be a form of competition wherein you quite frequently become the center of attention. This choice of behavior can be an effective manner in which to control the way others react to you.

CONTROL-EMOTE BEHAVIOR

You describe yourself as being more emoting and less controlling. You view yourself as a warm and open person whom others will applaud as the source of a lighthearted and friendly atmosphere. You find you gain more of a following from this approach than you would if you were to be cold and demanding of others. You see dealing with details as a burden to be avoided. It is more pleasant to encourage interactions in which others will assume that responsibility.

GETTING THE JOB DONE

Some of your decisions are based on gut feelings which do not require a lot of outside validation. Your spontaneity often influences others to act without delay.

You see as a creative approach which stimulates the willing cooperation of others who may look to you for some form of inspiration. You take pride in your ability to persuade others to accept you and your point of view and work hard at obtaining this acceptance.

In working with others, you will be frustrated when they cause delay by taking time to assure themselves that a course of action is comfortable. To you, their data gathering is largely unnecessary in making such a choice.

A good choice will validate itself as you go along with it-a bad choice can be discarded. You will also find it difficult to tolerate situations where there is little positive response to, or recognition for, an exciting idea.

Alternatively, your need for personal recognition can give people the impression you put your own ideas that you pay little attention to others' thoughts. You offer opinions readily, but can give the feeling you are expressing ideas and attitudes *"off the top of your head."* Thus, you can appear disorganized and ill-prepared in situations calling for a systematic approach.

BUILD ON YOUR ASSETS

Your behavior pattern can be a source of excitement and stimulation to others. Seek to use it well by keeping it properly tuned to the audience to whom you are playing. Remember that not everything is as exciting to others as it is to you.

Constant cheerleading can be viewed as overwhelming if not insincere. Also, your expressive approach can be seen as either refreshingly carefree or careless. Be sure to pay appropriate attention to the facts of a situation even though they are dull and uninteresting.

You can improve your interpersonal effectiveness by being a careful about your spontaneous comments. Your cheers and approval of others will be appreciated and will motivate cooperation; but jeers and *"zingers"* can turn fun-intended comments into a cause for others to downgrade your participation.

SOCIAL STYLE SELF-PERCEPTION "AMIABLE STYLE"

ASK-TELL BEHAVIOUR

Your self-description shows you see yourself as more asking and less telling. This probably relates to being willing to let others have their say, making an extra effort to support to group efforts rather than take controversial stand and be disruptive. You take time to be sure your participation is in accord with the existing agenda, and you can be helpful to anyone who needs support in that same cause.

CONTROL-EMOTE BEHAVIOUR

You describe yourself as being more emoting and less controlling. You see yourself as being sensitive to the feeling and emotions expressed by others. It is part of your approach to encourage them to be as open in revealing their feelings as you are.

You prefer to work with others where there are good feelings; you seek to foster working closing with people and are stimulated by the discoveries you make about them personally.

GETTING THE JOB DONE

Your manner of working with others on a task is largely a matter of being cooperative, and you feel you are skilled in gaining this cooperation through building relationships. Your commitment to others is strong, and you will expend a great deal of energy in meeting your obligations to them.

You are willing to take quite a lot of responsibility for helping others get along in working together. You likely experience consideration discomfort when pushed to participate in an interaction in a way you feel may be destructive to the basic relationship involved. You may prefer to go with the flow rather than deal with the tension such action will bring out.

When others are upset, you prefer to with that problem rather than moving on and ignoring it. You might have difficulty taking an independent or personal stand when the job demands it. There, more aggressive people may feel they can easily override you because you appear to accept their ideas readily.

Other also feels you will avoid or overlook conflict, and such seeming acquiescence may make it possible for people to ignore you. You seem to have difficulty taking the initiative to build recognition for yourself and are often seen as preferring to work in the background.

BUILD ON YOUR ASSETS

Your friendly and helpful style can earn you the support of others in return. Use your sensitivity to other as a measure with which you can determine the need to be aware of undesirable feelings which might be evolving. Be sure you are not being overly sensitive to feelings that are not significant to the situation.

People will enjoy your warmness and friendliness and it can open doors for you, if you are willing to capitalize on it. It will be important to your credibility to develop a willingness to open in stating what you think on a given issue without so much concern for the tension this plainness might create. You might find this easier to do if you learn to use a questioning, or *"devil's advocate,"* approach to depersonalize the process.

Develop ways to help yourself move into an interaction more forcefully. Perhaps, at first, just speaking up sooner is more important than seeking to speak with force.

YOUR STYLE IS NOT YOUR WHOLE PERSONALITY

Many people would like to refer behavioral style as personality but the truth is your personality is multidimensional in nature than the behavioral style, it encompasses your hope, your values, your intelligence, your dreams, and these things are what make you unique, though your behavioral style is not the totality of your personality but it is really very important in life.

SOCIAL STYLE SELF-PERCEPTION

Not necessarily worse. Not necessarily better. But different. Behaviorally speaking, you're in the minority. Every individual is (*Robert Bolton and Dorothy Grover Bolton in People Style at Work*) 75% of the population is significantly different from you.

These people, many of whom are important to your success. Everyone as long as you are human being, you possess a style to which you relate to people, to a very large extent the population of the world is significantly different from you, many of these people are very important when it comes to helping you attain your dreams.

They are important because they:

Think Differently

Use time differently

Deal with conflicting opinions Differently

Mange stress differently

Work at a different pace

Communicate differently

Handle emotions differently

Pretty much it is of interest to really relate to us about what makes this difference possible by explaining and properly analyzing the strength in these different styles. There are four different styles, it will be helpful you study the four of them then know the one that matches your personality, and also you will find how to maximize your style.

Large Source of this chapter was gotten from: Connections; My Guide; The Sheraton Experience.

CHAPTER TEN

POWER OF LOVE

According to Stephanie Dowrick, *"Love means wishing others to be happy. Love is about what we give not what we get?" "Love is not love except when it is generous."*

Unlocking your love power is like activating your creative ability. Loving humanity will simply reward you at the long run, it is naturally and the Master Mind designed life that way and it's my pleasure to unveil to you this mystery of life.

Have you ever seen a movie titled "*Robinson Crusoe*" if you've not seen the movie, you might have read the book but if you haven't seen both then know today that he had a ship wreck and he found himself in a deserted island and no one to talk to but the first time he saw Sam, he was amazed at how gorgeous, incredible reflection of God's image and likeness.

And in normal circumstance if Robinson Crusoe had seen that same man in England he would be indifferent. We tend to take people for nothing most especially when there are various classes of people to choose from and even at that class, we usually get bored of them. Loving humanity is necessary for our wellbeing.

THINK OF LOVE AS AN ACTION AND NOT A FEELING

A feeling is something we get from people, and when its ceases then we fail to reciprocate love our own love. And when such feelings fail to exist we often change our attitude towards the person or people we have feelings for, the feelings we get when we act in a certain way becomes our reward from people and if the feelings becomes negative we get irritated at them.

But if we still continue to show love in spite of how it makes us feel or our benefit then we have started loving. As you continue, you will cultivate love in your subconscious mind.

When we continuously show kindness, compassion and care in spite of what we'll get from, it is love put to action. Feeling can be what you owe your spouse but you must show the whole world love. Sympathy is Feeling as empathy is to love. The difference maybe the action empathy projects.

HOW TO START LOVING

We found out that your soul is too precious to be denied love; we design these techniques to unlock your power of love. The reason why some of us don't show love is probably due to our perception of love, past experiences and so on. From now onward as long as you have a deep desire to love, these techniques will activate your ability to love again.

LOVE CREATION

Though loving human is a necessity, you have to start from somewhere, as long as you would like to love humanity the starting point to the unlocking your power to love is to firstly love nature, because nature is God. It will be beautiful if we love other things like trees, animals and the sky, the bright day; loving creation totally will activate your desire to start loving humanity from the moment you sincerely open up your heart to doing this. In our busy schedules day after day it will go a long way if we take time out to appreciate the ability of man to communicate, to accomplish; and man's creative powers, we should acknowledge this wonderful gadget. As we appreciate these wonderful abilities, it goes a long way to connect us with nature which naturally activates our power to love.

DESIGN A VIRTUE LIST

In order to see the beauty in humanity focus on their virtues not really what they look like, focus on their point of strength and not weakness. Commence by making list of their glaring virtues, those nice things that are desirable in them.

Find time to identify and analyze how the people we enjoy their company were able to put smiles on our face, watch out for these in other people, do not make money or appearance your point of focus, you can relate with anyone, learn to put pride at bar because pride is the enemy of love.

In your virtue list, distinguish between one virtue from the other, still prioritize them identifying which is better than the other. To enable you figure this out, I designed a virtue list to aid you.

Mature

Methodical

Moral

Wise

Skillful

Sweet

Optimistic

Persistent

Punctual

Scholarly

Thrift

Organized

Polite

Practical

Realistic

Skillful

Tolerant

Original

Relaxed

Spiritual

Versatile

Neat

Open

Productive

Reliable

Sweet

Warm

Talented

Zealous

Agreeable

Articulate

Calm

Charitable

Conscientious

Decisive

Efficient

Fair

Gentle

Honest

Knowledgeable

Altruistic

Assertive

Caring

Cheerful

Consistent,

Cooperative

Creative

Decisive

Dignified

Energetic

Flexible

Humble

Handy

Diplomatic

Enthusiastic

Forgiving

Hardworking

Idealistic

Logical

Easy-going

Friendly

Expressive

Generous

Healthy

Loyal

Loving

LOOK BEYOND THE WRONG

It would be of benefit to us if we utilize our energy and every opportunity to focus on the virtues of our neighbors, lecturers, relatives, boss, employees and customers etc. Then we can realize the good things about them and see reasons to start associating with them. We make major mistake in life by focusing on people's faults.

Remember you have the ability to checkmate what enters your mind and if you really want to love then let only the virtues of people be where your mind is fixed on and not their wrongs and you will definitely see reasons to love them again.

Every human is intelligent and full of potential, bubbling with vitality. If all things becomes equal all men will be good because they have conscience that reminds them of all their wrong and they will feel remorse about that wrongs, so look beyond the wrongs and relate.

No matter how low a human being had sunk there is still an important virtue of potential within him or her: he is rational and capable to make some reasonable decision and this is an important gesture that separates a man and animal. Don't forget that he is endowed with an unlimited mind which produces virtues with equal potentials because there is no greater virtue and lower virtue.

TO LOVE OR BE LOVED

Right in your mind, there is an important question that is ringing a bell and if i don't give answers to this question it would he better I never attached power of love in this book. Your question is what if they never love back? Using the "*devil's advocate*" I will allow you to answer the question yourself by asking you "which one carries the greater pleasure: to give love or to be loved?

Giving out love is greater because it shows you've understood the love concept and you can now manufacture unlimited love to give away to all.

Victor Moses a Nigerian footballer had his parents killed at the Niger-Delta crisis of 2002 in Nigeria, which had the Federal government fully involved because military men were deployed to the region which got many Niger-Deltans killed and Victor Moses' parents become victims among those murdered, and that happen at his tender age but when he was grow up he ventured into football and was called upon to play for that same country whose military men killed his parents, he focused his mind on the virtues and not faults which made him contribute greatly to the success of Super Eagles that won African Nations cup of January 2013.

You can never imagine how influential you will be by unlocking your soul to love other souls because every soul wants to connect. Victor Moses got connected to his people and just because of his decision; it made Nigerians love him the more. When you perceive someone's deep virtues I mean their honesty, compassion and intelligence then will you be able to share in their beauty.

At the deepest depth of the struggle to love is the conflict between the soul and the bod, the body will always class people then choose those that marches its class but the souls yearn to relate and to see the best in others. We read our spiritual book which says that the Master Mind loves every soul, He loved every soul because to him every soul is equal. And as perfect as the Master Mind is, He saw all of us as equal, then what about you that is one of His offsprings.

We are living in a society where class come to play but little did we know that those people we call low class are also humans like us. Elevate your conscious; become godlike by loving others irrespective of the veneer they come with.

Mind you, our ego contradicts our zeal to relate with people, it often want us to look at their class, when we focus on class, we will begin to see the fault being popped up. To relate with people is either by looking not at people's faults and their classes but by loving them in a creative way.

TO LOVE IS TO BE CREATIVE

A man or woman that loves humanity will be embodied with the ability to connect to the Master Mind who reveals to him strategies to help humanity and the end result will be a super man or woman who is powerful beyond measures because he did the first thing first by putting humanity first. The Bible said seek you first the kingdom of God and every other things shall be added unto you. Seeking God's kingdom is practically loving humanity.

But if on getting to the top you tend to forget your source, you will be brought down for he said pride leads to a man's down fall. This is the secret of the world richest people. BILL GATE gives aid to Africa, South American, and Caribbean etc., just because he knows what it takes to love.

His love towards humanity gave him the sound ideas to manufacture Microsoft to make work easier for mankind and he is being celebrated for just loving human. The reward of loving humanity is creative beyond measures and there lies the secret of celebrated inventors.

Are you still asking the same question or is it how to start? The beginning can be frustrating, it might seems difficult that you would rather want to quit but as we all know that had it been Michael Faraday quitted in his love for humanity, he wouldn't have had the sound idea to make sure you change your phones, watch television and operate laptops.

You may say another person would have come up with the same idea, no one might knew how long it might take for another to possess such lofty idea and beside, that other mind that would bear such idea would be a mind that loved humanity.

Thomas Eddison hated darkness and he gave us a light bulb because he had lobe in his heart, for without love no man could think of light in the midst of darkness. Start loving now so that the biggest ideas to transform the world would come to you. You can now see the reason to love and not to care if you are loved or not.

UNITY IN LOVE

We are getting the ultimate benefit of loving humanity and knowing this will elevate us to the highest pinnacles of wisdom because the wisest King that ever lived King Solomon knows this. He asked for the understanding to rule his people and wisdom and riches was added, but your motive shouldn't be to love for the benefit of getting wealthy, it should be pure and true for the effect to take place.

Think of everyone in the world as a connecting to each other in a wider view irrespective of the colour, if the process of reproduction was true as it is then you will agree with me that humanity started from one parents.

Take for instance, if you harm yourself on the course of slicing onion, will you use the other hand to cut the hand that harmed you? No of course. Why? Because the other hand is a part of you. When you see humanity as a part of you, revenge becomes ridiculous.

Life is spiritual and shouldn't be viewed only from the physical view point alone. The physical tells us that we are divisive and are separated but viewing life spiritually will reveal to you that people who are more united and loved themselves always come out the best in everything in life.

I was watching one of the X-FACTOR TV REALITY SHOW and I observed a team in less coherence state because they lack love, I've also seen dances like samba, in such dance if one of the dancers is actually indifferent then that dance will be a flop.

See the world from the field of play probably American football, if one person scores then the team wins regardless of who scored as long as the team wins, these mindset will spur creativity in the playground. 2014 world cup analyst saw the Brazilian team to be playing like a "*happy family*" because they were bounded by love.

The game of life is not based on individual win, it is not a zero sum game, it must be a win-win or else you are putting your peace of mind in the run.

In FC Barcelona everyone trusts the ability of Messi to score goals; this will make his team always release the ball to him if he is in a better position to score. If one player scores a winning goal then the whole team wins.

See everyone as part of your team fighting together against challenges and unseen forces against humanity, let the love in your heart spur you up to map our ways to help mankind out of its problems.

When we look at everyone as one, even if the other guy is wiser and is richer he will be willing to share his wisdom and we both will become even wiser because we are connected irrespective of background or colour.

In the school environment even as a student, if i find any topic difficult, i would have no fear because am sure someone will willing teach me and that will foster corporation and enhance unity. We will become healthier and also learn much better in a lovely environment where everyone is themselves as one, this brood progressiveness.

It is only love that is potent enough to heal the world and make it a better place for human species, animals and trees. So let's start loving.

LOVE BEGINS AT HOME

Where is the love when men who claim to love humanity, still maltreat their wife, husband, children and siblings, are mere hypocrites and bunch of liars. If you claim you love humanity and your house is on fire then you will have to read this chapter very well, digest it and use it firstly at home before anywhere else because a popular seeing says "*charity begins at home.*"

For one to be qualified to even say that he loves humanity then he must make progressions in showing love to family members ranging from parent, siblings, spouse and then to children.

The main purpose of these is to love others as much as we love our siblings, parents and children. Matrimony is a good training ground because in the home you see your spouse as you see yourself.

Love to your child is giving him or her quality time; attend their shows, go to the beach or movies with them, attend their end of the year programs; don't let money chasing come in-between you and your family.

Don't alienate yourself from your spouse, your children; infact become their best friends. Try to go back to that virtue page and give a smile of appreciation to yourself before you show it on anyone you sincerely decide to love then continue till you love them all and encourage yourself for working toward acquiring such power to love but most especially take pleasure in your strength at least for your ability to access yourself and being able to unlock your love power so start being creative.

AS YOU THINKETH SO IT IS

King Solomon told us that "*As a man thinketh in his heart so is he*" and also what we think about other people determines how we treat them. If you think your brother as a stranger from that day that's what he will become to you and if you think your neighbor as your brother, then from that day upward your thinking of him as a neighbor eludes your mind and you will start seeing him as a brother.

Whatever you think affects the way you feel which determines your action. If you are in a place and someone enters, whatever you think about the person affects the way you relate with the person, if you think the person as a brother then you will influence him to take you as a brother also. When a lady or a gent enters a room, do you always want to pull back or do you want to relate with them and it all begins in your perception of them which is shaped by thought.

When you talk to others as strangers that is what they will always be. Develop the habit of seeing other people as your brother or sister (*without sounding patronizing /then you will find it much easier to love them*) and also influence them to do the same.

LOVE IS NOT COMFORT AT ALL TIME

Love doesn't mean making people or expecting people to always treat you the way you want, it does not entail comfort at all times, love is not letting people have their way both good and bad either, for that will breed manipulation. Love also entail rebuke and corrections too.

In fact if anyone you love does anything wrong call them back with love and correct them without hesitation, letting them have their way is not love at all.

There is no way you would want them to go the painful lane when you know for sure that pain will result to their gain at the long run if they don't negate your chastisement. If correcting people is painful to them, then remind them that there is a price for everything, those pains will enable them to grow in character as human.

Let me close this book by saying to you all to keep the loving alive. It's been a wonderful moment. I love you more.

Contact me if this book touched your life in any way
(*Email: michaelmbuko@gmail.com*
fb: Michael Mbuko
Facebook page: Michael Ugochukwu Mbuko)

Michael U. Mbuko

ABOUT THE BOOK

You are not an ordinary being! You were born with unique capacity and ability that is out of this world. You have all it takes to make every vision possible and make a success that is impacting the whole world meaningfully.

You are loaded beyond the depth of your imagination; you are carrying something special for this generation. You are a Superstar! You can fulfill your purpose for living, experience greater fulfillment and contribute to the growth and development of the world, more importantly its success.

Great author of our time, Michael U. Mbuko teaches you strategies and skills that will enable you to unlock your hidden powers in order to go over big and get to the top of the ladder in this life.

This masterpiece will empower you to make the best of your inherent abilities and play by different set of rules to be completely different in this life. This life-giving masterpiece will inspire you to succeed fully.

It will get you loaded with the courage of your convictions to be ahead of the game and streets ahead of

176

others. Wouldn't you rather be the most important person where you live and become extremely successful?

It is time to hit the mark and leave your mark. You cannot afford to settle for less when you can have all things working for you. Move mountains and be the leading light that lightens up the world.

You are a high flier; discover the wisdom you really need to unlock your hidden powers now and create a presence that will continue to grow beyond your lifetime. This paperback unveils to you, the wisdom to unlock your hidden powers.

ABOUT THE AUTHOR

Michael U. Mbuko is a leading authority in human development, he is committed in making sure humanity discover their fullest self thus becoming effective in the society. May be that is the reason he has spoken vividly about self-mastery and is promising to write many prize winning books and so much more centered on self-actualization, relationship and leadership.

Michael is also the President of Concerned Youths for the Less-Privileged International; an NGO triggered with the responsibility of re-orienting the mindset of youths round the world. He is a Political Scientist and analyst, alumni of the Prestigious Obafemi Awolowo University Ile-Ife Nigeria. He holds BSc. (*Honors*) in Political Science.

www.ingramcontent.com/pod-product-compliance
Lightning Source LLC
La Vergne TN
LVHW041317080426
835513LV00008B/505